M000238947

Red Clay and Dust:
The Evolution of Southern Dirt Racing

Gary L. Parker

WALDENHOUSE PUBLISHERS, INC.
WALDEN, TENNESSEE

Red Clay and Dust: The Evolution of Southern Dirt Racing
Copyright 2015 © Gary L. Parker. All rights reserved.
No part of this book may be reproduced in any form or by any electronic or
mechanical means including information storage and retrieval systems, without
permission in writing from the author. The only exception is by a reviewer,
who may quote short excerpts in a review.
Front cover art by Kent Harrelson.
ISBN: 978-1-935186-61-8
Library of Congress Control Number: 2015911265
Published by Waldenhouse Publishers, Inc.
100 Clegg Street, Signal Mountain, Tennessee 37377 USA
www.waldenhouse.com   888-222-8228
Printed in the United States of America

Acknowledgments

There are so many people to thank who contributed in various ways to the writing of this book. There are the late model drivers and their families who gave me their valuable time. The track owners, that allowed me to come and collect the histories and photograph their facilities. The people who provided photos, articles, programs, and stories, I want to tell them thanks for the important part their efforts played in this book.

A number of people I owe a special thanks to. Those include, Katy Boyd Coulter, Elmer "Butch" Boyd, Robert Walden, Rocky Estes, Tommy Hickman, Chris Corum, Chris Tilley, Kevin Coffey, Clint Elkins, Gene Stinson, Brad Hendricks, Leon Sells, Jody Ridley, Danny Hedrick, Buster Vineyard, Lynn Acklin, David "Peanut" Jenkins, and Jeff Smith.

Then there are those whose help I could not have completed this book without. Nick Nicholson, who was always there with a photograph just when I was about to give up on finding it. Deborah Perry, for her help with the history of Cherokee Speedway. Longtime Toccoa Speedway announcer, Charles Head, for his help in filling in some of the blanks in Toccoa Speedway's long history. Debra Swims, for her assistance with the section on her late husband, Mike's Hav-A-Tampa Series. Michael Motes for his help on the history of Atomic and Smoky Mountain Speedways. Finally, a very special thanks to Kent Harrelson for his hard work on the book's cover. Kent was able to get my vision of the cover into his head and design it just as I thought it would look.

There are many others who made a contribution to this book in some way and I wish to thank you also. Finally. I want to think the entire Southern late model dirt racing world for just being there for me and the thousands of others to enjoy through the years and for the many years to come. THANK YOU.

Introduction

My love for dirt racing began one Friday night in the late Fall of 1955. At the age of six, my dad took me to my first dirt race at the famed Boyd's Speedway in Chattanooga, Tennessee. To this day I still remember quite a bit about the race. Most of the cars racing that night were of the jalopy category. I recall the car that took the checkered flag was a white Ford fender-less jalopy that sported the red number one on its side. I believe "Wild Man" Jerry Smith was the driver of that car.

Since then I have watched hundreds of races all over the South. At race tracks that included: the Cherokee Speedway in Gaffney, South Carolina; Dixie Speedway and the Rome Speedway in Georgia; the tiny quarter-mile Spring City Raceway, the Volunteer Speedway, and the legendary Smokey Mountain Speedway in Tennessee; to the Green Valley Speedway in Alabama. These are but a few of the tracks I have traveled to over the last sixty years.

Also, I have witnessed races at several historic tracks, which sadly, no longer exist. Among them, the famed Atomic Speedway outside of Knoxville, Tennessee; and Lakewood Speedway (known as the Indy of the South), located at the old state fairgrounds in south Atlanta; the Canton International Speedway located near Canton, Georgia; and finally, the old round bowl known as Turner Speedway (the old mountain) in Cummings, Georgia. At this track the race cars did what was then known as "The Cummings Slide" (race cars stayed in a power slide all the way around the track).

During my many years of involvement with dirt racing, I traveled and became close friends with some of the icons of Southern dirt racing including, Jody Ridley, and H.E. (Doc) Vineyard. Over the years I helped these two drivers in the pits. I was a member of Ridley's crew from the late 60's through all of the 70's. Then was part of Vineyard's pit crew for several years in the 80's.

My passion for dirt racing will always be with me. I have seen a lot of technological changes in dirt late model cars over a sixty year span. However, I feel certain the technology will keep rapidly changing into the future. You might call what I have a "racing addiction," something that will never go away. Just ask any true dirt late model race fan; or the drivers who propel these 800+hp race cars around the red clay tracks with that familiar "rooster" tail of dust following behind.

I was asked many times over the years to write this book. I only wish I had written the book earlier when some of the great drivers of the sport were still with us. Drivers like, Tootle Estes, Buck Simmons, Scott Sexton, and others who could have put their valuable thoughts and insights into the book.

The purpose of the book--Red Clay and Dust: The Evolution of Southern Dirt Racing—will be to focus on the race cars known as "late models" or "super late models." We begin with a short history of the earliest days of automobile racing in the South. Then we look at the first dirt late models of the late-50's. Then our focus shifts to the evolution of the super late models, from the earliest late models, to those that race today's red clay dirt tracks.

Next we take a look to a number of dirt racing series that have operated or are operating in the Southeast. We begin with the forerunner of all late model dirt series, the National Dirt Racing Association (NDRA) and its colorful founder and promoter Robert Smawley. Then attention shifts to the Hav-A-Tampa Dirt Racing Series, with its famous Hav-A-Tampa Shootouts held annually at the Dixie Speedway in Woodstock, Georgia. Next, we look at the longest running regional dirt late model series, the Southern All-Stars Racing Series and its founder B.J. Parker. Finally, we take a look at the Lucus Oil Late Model Dirt Series, a national series that races throughout the country, with a number of stops in the South. Our focus then shifts to a number of dirt tracks throughout the South, with their colorful histories and their contributions to dirt racing.

Attention then goes to the late model drivers, a number of them from the past (some sadly no longer with us). Finally, we look at some of the "dirt warriors" currently running the dirt tracks of the South, using words, interviews, stories, and photos to introduce them to you the race fan.

I hope you enjoy reading this book as much as I have enjoyed researching and writing it. Late model dirt racing will always be my "addiction." I hope it becomes your addiction too.

Gary L. Parker

Contents

Red Clay & Dust

CHAPTER ONE:

A SHORT HISTORY OF DIRT RACING BEFORE THE LATE MODEL

Dirt racing's roots can be traced back to the invention of the automobile and competitive auto racing itself. The sport had its birth in the South as early as 1917 at Atlanta's historic Lakewood Speedway, located at the old state fairgrounds in South Atlanta. The first race at the speedway was a match race between big time rivals at the time, Barney Oldfield and Ralph DePalma, witnessed by a crowd of over 15,000 race fans. During the 1920's and up until the mid-1940's one must keep in mind that most dirt races in the South and other parts of the country were racing cars known as "big cars." These race cars were early versions of the "open-wheel" sprints cars. "Big cars" continued to evolve throughout this time period, becoming faster and more sophisticated with each passing year. .

In the 1930's Ralph Hankinson, a young sales representative with White Rock Water Company, located in Whitestone, New York, with the help of a sanctioning body known as the American Automobile Association(AAA), began bargaining with fair officials all over the South. The result was, that in 1935 a number of dirt races were held at such sites as, the South Carolina State Fair in Columbia; the Florida State Fair in Tampa; and the North Carolina State Fair in Raleigh to name a few. Hankinson continued to promote AAA sanctioned races all over the country until his death in 1942.

Another pioneering auto racing promoter was J. Alex Sloan of Pittsburgh, Pennsylvania. In 1905 Sloan began promoting auto races, even before Ralph Hankinson. In 1915 the International Motor Contest Association (IMCA) was organized by Sloan. By the time of his death in 1937, Sloan had promoted more auto races than all other promoters in the United States.

After Sloan's death his son John A. Sloan Jr. continued his father's promotion business. John Jr. changed the operating name to Racing Corporation of America. He was able to maintain the promoting success his father had achieved in the North, but especially in the South. For example, in 1937 the Racing Corporation of America held a number of IMCA racing events at several sites in the South. Among them were, the Alabama State Fair in Birmingham, Alabama; the Mid-South State Fair in Memphis, Tennessee; and the Tri-State Fair in Chattanooga, Tennessee. Finally, under John Sloan's watch IMCA held its first late model race on November 9, 1947 in Lubbock, Texas.

A new type of race car was introduced to Southern race fans in the 1940's. "Midget" race cars began invading the South. Midget Racing had long been popular among the Northern race fans. However, north of the Mason-Dixon line the racing season was of a much shorter duration due to the early onslaught of cold weather. Southern race fans soon found a new type of racing to compete with "big car" racing, popular among Southern race fans for decades. Thus, the midget racing teams came south for no other reason than to escape the cold weather and to extend their racing season.

As a result, a number of visionary race promoters began organizing midget racing circuits in several Southern states, such as Alabama, Georgia, Florida, and Tennessee. Perhaps the best known of these were, the Southern States Racing Association, financed by several Atlanta businessmen. These Atlanta promoters conducted races in Birmingham, Atlanta, and Chattanooga. Another popular midget circuit was Southern States Speedways. This series ran a number of races in Florida shortly after World War II. Finally, the Mason-Dixon Racing Circuit held a number of midget races in the border states of Virginia and Maryland.

After the Hankinson's, one the best known racing promoters was a skinny and bespectacled man known as Sam Nunis of Cedartown, Georgia. Shortly after World War I Nunis became a race car driver in Ralph Hankinson's Traveling Big Car Races, which toured the country's county fair circuit. However, in 1926 Sam's racing career came to an end in a serious crash at a track in Concord, North Carolina. After a long recovery Nunis became

Ralph Hankinson's assistant and the next 10 years were spent learning to promote races.

Shortly after World War II Nunis promoted car races up and down the East coast, and into the South as well. Sam had a unique way of persuading first radio, and then television stations to cover his events. In the mid-1940's he organized the National Stock Car Racing Association that predated NASCAR.

Sam promoted several Southern races, including a number of races at the famed "one mile dirt oval" known as Lakewood Speedway south of Atlanta.

Sam Nunis left as the promoter of Trenton Speedway in Trenton, New Jersey and retired in 1973. Sadly Nunis died in 1980 in Florida due to heart and lung disease.

As we have noted, the first half of the 20th Century featured oval track car racing being staged on horse racing tracks of a half mile or more. These tracks were usually located at state or county fairs. During the period two types of cars were raced: "big cars" and midgets.

However, the winds of change started to take place in auto racing in the late 1940's and into the 1950's. These changes were twofold in nature. The first, racing on fairgrounds horse tracks began to decline for two major reasons. It became clear the wooden posts and fences were a danger to both the spectators and the race car drivers. Secondly, the dust created at these tracks was blinding to the spectators watching the events; but especially dangerous to the drivers trying to see the other race cars. For example, Lakewood Speedway had a number of racing deaths attributed to the blinding dust. Perhaps the best known of these racing deaths occurred in 1946. At the Labor Day race that year George Barrington and, the Indy 500 winner that year, George Robson were killed as a result of the horrendous dust.

As a result, in the late 1940's and into the 1950's came a rise in the number of purpose-built tracks (tracks built specifically for auto racing) throughout the United States. This was very evident in the South. Among the Southern tracks that started to appear were; the Peach Bowl (1949) in Atlanta, Georgia; Broadway Speed-way (1949) in Knoxville, Tennessee; Boyd's Speedway (1952) in Chattanooga, Tennessee; Golden Strip Speedway (1954) in Fountain Inn, South Carolina; the Toccoa Speedway (1955) in Toccoa, Georgia; the Athens Speedway (1958) in Athens, Georgia; and finally, Cherokee Motor Speedway (also known as Sutalee-1959) in Canton, Georgia to name but a few. Thus, we have witnessed the first wind of change in auto racing, the shift to purpose-built race tracks.

This Modified is one type of race car that ran before the first late models in the mid-60's. (Photo Courtesy of "Little" Bill Corum)

The second wind of change was the rise of race cars known as "stock cars" and their early cousin, the "jalopy." The early versions of stock cars and/or the jalopy were the fender-less 1930's and 1940's era street cars. Stock cars raced sporadically in the 1930's on a number of dirt track's racing programs.

In 1940 a publicist, working for a mid-west racing association best described auto racing's potential in the area of "stock car" racing. He said: "Many people would rather see a car they know something about race, than the mysterious motors that cost more than a W.P.A. project. Many owners that cannot afford to put that kind of money in a sport can afford a stock car, and they get speed from mechanical ability, not by buying it." The rise of the purpose-built tracks increased the interest in stock car racing. Most local drivers could not afford the cost of a "big car" or a midget racer, but could manage the cost of a stock car. Many a local race drivers got their stock car racing start at the local "junk" yard. Home-built stock cars quickly took root. This was especially true in the South where junk yards had plenty of junked cars, "good ole boy" drivers, and a lot of red clay to race on.

We have taken a short look at early auto racing in the United States. Our focus was mainly on the South. In the next chapter we will take a look at the evolution of the "late" model from its earliest forms in late-50's; to the rear steer driven "super" late models that dominate the dirt tracks of our nation, and especially those dirt tracks of the South.

CHAPTER TWO:
THE EVOLUTION OF THE DIRT LATE MODEL

Today's dirt late model race fans, watching their favorite driver's rear steer, 800+ hp super late model scream down the straightaways; then pitch violently into the turns, a rooster tail of dust and red clay spraying from the rear tires; have little idea of the evolution that has changed these wicked machines since the late 1950's. The hulled out 1939 Ford coupes, the 1950 Fords, Plymouths, the Hudson Hornets, and the 1955-56 Chevrolets and Fords have given way, over the years, to the super late models we see on the Southern dirt tracks today.

Jody Ridley in a typical "home built" race car. (Photo courtesy of Jody Ridley)

Beginning in the late 1950's, steel, full-bodied cars, like those mentioned above, were either bought new (a lucky few) or found at a junkyard. These cars were brought home, hulled out and built into the first of what we now call "late model" stock car. Most often, the home-built late model of this period was constructed at the driver or crew member's home or small garage. These early race cars were first hulled out (unnecessary parts removed to lighten the car), glass removed, and steel rollcages welded into the car's interior. The driver's side door had added bars for additional safety.

The suspension systems were stiff, especially the right side suspension. At the time, one of the most common suspension systems used a heavy duty 31/44 ton truck spring. Other early systems used leaf spring set-ups (wide leaf springs were very popular).

Let us now take a look at the early late model race engines. These early engines had a 60 to 85hp range. Sometimes a good master mechanic could squeeze almost 200hp out of an engine. Race engines continued to change throughout the 1950's into the mid-1960's. Most of these race engines were modified stock engines, often bored 10 to 30 over. The cubic inch displacement (cid) of these engines, ranged from 283 up to the 427 (cid). For example, Jody Ridley and Fred Cook used a 289 (cid) in their early 1956 Fords. Others like Harold Fryar and Bob Burcham used a 283 (cid) in their 1955 Chevrolets. The larger engines, the 327(cid) up to the mighty 427 (cid) were used in the mid-1960's up to the early 1970's. I remember Tootle Estes used a 427 (cid) engine in the yellow Ford Fairlane # 28 he drove in the mid-1960's at Smoky Mountain Speedway. Finally, no race fan can forget Jody Ridley's 1964 Ford Falcon #98 which most often ran a 302 (cid) engine. He had over 61 Feature wins one year with this race car. This was pretty much the late model dirt engine scene until the appearance of the "after-market" engines in the 1970's.

So, the period between the late 1950's until the end of the 1960's could be called, "the home-built late model era." During this period, we witness a number of changes to the dirt race car. Perhaps the major change was the fender-less jalopies evolving into stock appearing race cars, the 1955-56 Chevrolets and the 1956 Ford come to mind.

At this time there were: no "bought" race cars, no "bought" race engines, no factory support, and very little, if any, "after-

Typical early late model a 1956 Ford. (Photo courtesy of Robbie Henry)

market" parts available for use on these early late models. Also, race damage to the car's body was repaired and painted by a paint and body man. Most of the engines were built and repaired by a local mechanic. Body and engine parts were most often found at the local junkyard. If a special part and/or parts were needed for the engine or chassis you had to employ the services of a machinist. Even the car number and the name of the sponsors had to be painted on the car (Fred Grooms lettered hundreds of race cars in the Chattanooga area), thus a talented sign painter was needed (no vinyl decals at this time). As you can see, the early late models required a lot of time and hard work to keep them racing.

The late 1960's until the mid-1970's saw the evolutionary process in dirt late models gain momentum. All across the South and other parts of the country small race shops sprang up. The shops began constructing late model dirt cars on specific factory-made frames.

Dirt track race fans were introduced to a new type of late model. These new dirt machines were crafted from mid-size factory cars and a few sporty high performance cars of the time. The shops removed the glass, sealed the doors, took out the lights and sealed the holes they left with sheet metal. Except for the big racing tires, these dirt late model race cars still looked stock in appearance.

The Ford late model drivers preferred the 1963-68 Fairlanes, the 1964-65 Falcon, and the 1965-69 Mustang. However, the Chevrolet drivers chose the 1967-78 Camaros, the 1968-72 Novas, and the 1963-72 Chevelles. Perhaps the best known Chevelle of the period was the famous gold and black #41 Chevelle driven by the legendary Buck Simmons. This car won numerous races throughout the South (especially at Dixie Speedway in Woodstock, Georgia) during the above mentioned time.

The legendary #41 Chevelle driven to so many wins by Buck Simmons. (Photo courtesy of Leon Sells)

As pointed out earlier, the late model chassis design of the period (late 1960's to mid-1970's) involved the shortening (usually 10 inches) of a full sized factory car frame (Ford Galaxie for example). Then the front steering and wheel systems were fabricated (A-arms upper/lower and safety hubs for example) and attached to the front of the shortened frame. This resulted in both a sturdy and durable racing chassis. At the time, this was the perfect racing chassis for attaching a late model car body, especially the uni-bodied race cars like the 1965 Ford Mustang Fastback.

The rear suspension systems of the late models continued to make use of the leaf spring systems of the earlier period. One of the most innovative changes was a rear suspension set up known to some as the "Reece Bar suspension system." Popular during the mid-70's and later, this system most often used two wide leaf springs (Chevy II leaf springs were popular) on each side of the rear axle. The Reece Bar was attached to a mount above the rear housing and then to the rear housing itself. This system worked well on "dry slick" dirt tracks. As the track dried out the Reece Bar forced the rear end and the suspension system to push against the track, thus reducing the spin of the tires. Doug Kenimer used this system in the early to late-70's to score a number of wins in his #42 Chevelle.

Finally, we take a look at the race engines of this period. For the most part, race engines were still being built by the local mechanic and/or the driver and his crew. Race engines continued to be modified stock engines. Most engine modifications consisted of engine bore (usually in the 10 to 30 over range). Sometimes different pistons, lifters, and cams were used to increase horsepower. Engine size also increased from the earlier period. The 327 (cid) and 350 (cid) engines were used in the Novas, Camaros, and Chevelles of the Chevrolet dirt drivers. The 302 (cid) and later a small number of 351 (cid) engines were used in the Fairlanes, Falcons, and Mustangs of the Ford drivers. The 302 (cid) was the main Ford dirt late model engine of the period and its smaller size,compared to the Chevrolet engines, required it turn more RPM's than its Chevy counterparts. As we see, not a lot of change in engine technology between the two periods of the late model dirt car. However, that was about to rapidly change as we approach the middle of the 1970's.

The biggest evolutionary explosion to date occurred in dirt late model racing in the 1970's. The mid-70's are often called the era of the "bought" race car. Almost the entire dirt late model car could now be bought and not fabricated in a small race shop. As a result, many "cottage" industries were born to service the growing late model racing industry. These new industries included the chassis builders and the after-market race engine builders. The pioneers in late model chassis and car design included, Jig-A-Low, Howe, and C.J. Rayburn. It was Rayburn that revolutionized the race suspension system with the "coil over" design. Also, Rayburn was one of the first to introduce disc brakes to dirt racing.

Another area the changed rapidly was the race engine scene. The race teams began turning to after-market race engines. For years race teams had built their own engines. However, as the late 70's and early 80's ushered in, a number of after-market race engine companies emerged. These companies were able to focus full time on engine research and development. As one race team after another started racing after-market engines, and winning big, other teams had to follow suit or be left behind. These early engine companies included, the pioneer in the field, Cornett Engines, located in Somerset, Kentucky. Other after-market engine companies were, Baker Engineering out of the mid-west, and Malcuit Racing engines, located in Strausburg, Ohio. Most of the engines being built at this time were in the 380 (cid) range and above, producing around 600 hp.

The late model race suspensions also underwent major changes during the latter part of the 70's. The growth in after-market shocks, coil springs, and in the 80's "coil overs," brought after-market suspension companies like Carrera, and Pro into the dirt racing scene.

Finally, the look of the late model dirt cars remained stock appearing. There was little change in the appearance of the late models racing in 70's to those that raced in the mid-60's. Perhaps, the only observable difference was the snub-nosed front ends that started to appear toward the end of the 1970's. These snub-nosed dirt cars were most often identified with Robert Smawley's National Dirt Racing Association (NDRA). This was the nation's first traveling dirt series, beginning in 1978. The race cars of choice remained the Novas, and Mustangs. However, the Chevrolet Camaros remained by far the most popular among the dirt late model drivers of the time.

The snub nose look of H. E. Vineyard's race car at Atomic Speedway. (Photo courtesy of H. E. Vineyard)

The 1980's witnessed the earliest stages of aerodynamics in dirt late models. The race cars adopted a sloped nose and roof design to go along with the rear spoiler. This sloping design created a down force on the car; creating a better handling race car, especially through the turns.

The most popular suspension system remained the leaf spring system of the earlier race cars. Most race teams still employed the Reece Bar system, mentioned earlier. As we discussed, after-market engines were starting to appear on the race scene. However, most engines were still "shop built" race engines. At the time, one of the most popular shop built engine was the Chevrolet Corvette 461-X double hump head power plant.

As the 80's progressed the dirt late model was about to radically evolve in appearance. The production steel bodies of past years were about to give way to first, the fiberglass bodies (a short lived period due to difficulty in repairing); then the fabricated sheet metal or molded component parts bodies.

In 1982 Charlie Swartz was about to change the look of the dirt late model forever. The dirt late models were about to become radically different from the earlier street appearing race cars. Swartz introduced what became known as the "wedge" late model. The cars were flat sided, longer, and almost a foot wider than the earlier race cars. In addition, these "wedge" cars had a large rear deck spoiler. They looked like a door stop that was going 100 mph when sitting still in the pits.

During the mid-80's wedge race teams were constantly experimenting ways to achieve more down force on the rear of the race car. This would produce what became known as the "lexan era" in dirt late model racing. Race teams constructed lexan sideboards off the car's rear deck and spoiler. Many outrageous looking configurations of lexan appeared on the wedge cars. Some teams went so far as to use whole sheets of lexan mounted off the driver's side to create down force and gain tire grip.

Lexan era Late model. (Photo courtsey of Nick Nicholson)

Because of their unique look, wedge late models became a fan favorite. However, they were gone about five years after they were first introduced at the Pennsboro Speedway in 1982. Two factors led to their demise: the high cost in building a wedge car, and safety concerns.

The dirt late models were dramatically down-sized in the late 80's. The wedge car's characteristic long, pointed nose remained a left-over fixture on dirt late models until the mid 90's. The next major evolutionary change in the late model body style occurred around 1994. The "stock appearing" nose would replace the pointed nose on the late models. Most of the race car's body shell was aluminum, with many improvements in body aerodynamics also taking place.

Before we go further, as the late model race cars became lighter and lighter in the 70's (some race teams were caught using muffler tail pipe for roll bars to make the cars lighter) many race tracks started requiring the cars to "make weight" in the late 70's. Today, late models (super late models) must weigh at least 2300 pounds with driver on board at the conclusion of a race.

The reason "making weight" was mentioned now is the next evolutionary stage in the late model body deals with today's "carbon fiber" body parts. Today's late models run carbon fiber (extremely light weight) body parts such as, hoods, side panels, roofs, and the MD3 Evolution Nose. Finally, the cars have V8 aluminum engines, aluminum rims, and a light weight 20 gallon fuel cell. This, along with the fiber carbon bodies and noses, makes today's super late model a 2300 pound light weight, aerodynamic red clay dirt monster.

In the last part of this chapter we take a look at the other two areas of focus in the evolution of the dirt late model; the suspension system, and the race engine. As we have seen, the leaf spring suspension system (especially the Reece Bar system) was the major system used. Toward the mid to late 80's early coil spring systems started to appear. In the early 90's fixed shock systems were popular among a number of drivers. Around 1995 a system known as the Four Bar Suspension system (bar angles to change rear suspension) became popular. Barry Wright Race Cars built late model cars that could use both the Four Bar or the leaf spring systems during the mid-90's. The late 90's saw the "coil over" shock (coil spring over the shock) revolution. The coil overs saw rapid changes in length and shorter valving, among the many innovations. This is one of the major areas of costs for today's race teams. The changes seen in coil over shock technology shows perhaps the greatest evolutionary change in dirt late model racing today.

Today's typical 2300 lb., 800+hp super dirt late model. (photo provided by Nick Nicholson)

Most super late model race teams today will tell you that the key to winning with a rear steer car is the suspension setup. The goal is to get the corner speed as fast as the straightaway speed. The front suspension is basically double A-arm with coil overs. The rear suspensions use either the Z-link (swing arm) and the more common Four-link systems. The adjustable systems of today's dirt super late model is an amazing work of technology, with five or more springs, track bars, sway bars, and swing arms. The bars can also be placed in a number of settings to enhance the race setup.

Our final look at the evolution of the dirt late model will involve the race engine. As mentioned earlier, the rise of the aftermarket engine industry continued to evolve through the 90's and into 2000's. The mid-90's saw the "open engine" rule appear in super late model racing. In addition to the aftermarket engine companies mentioned earlier, new players entered the super late model market. Among the new companies were Vic Hill Racing Engines, Pro Power Engines, Custom Race Engines, and the newly popular Roush Yates Racing Engines. Most of today's super late model engines are in the 380 cid to around 450 cid range, sport compression ratios in the mid-teens, use large four-barrel carbs, and produce between 800 and 900hp. Recently, Roush Yates has been testing their new RY45 race engine which has a horsepower range approaching 1000hp. Scott Bloomquist is probably the best known of the Roush Yates engine customers in super late model racing. Today's aftermarket race engines range in cost from the $40,000 to $62,000 range.

Finally, as the costs of engines, coil over shocks, chassis, tires and other racing parts continue to rise, one cannot help but see that it is really easy to buy speed these days. An old racer saying is never truer than it is today, "Speed costs money; how much speed do you want to buy?"

CHAPTER THREE:
LATE MODEL DIRT RACING SERIES THROUGH THE YEARS

This chapter takes a historical look at some of the dirt racing series that were and are currently instrumental to the Southern dirt late model scene. Beginning with the touring series that started it all, Robert Smawley's, National Dirt Racing Association (NDRA), which began in 1978. Next, our attention shifts to the Hav-A-Tampa Dirt Racing Series founded by, Mike Swims, and legendary race announcer Jimmy Mosteller. Also, the longest running regional dirt series, the Southern All-Stars Dirt Racing Series will be examined. In the final part of the chapter, the Lucas Oil Dirt Late Model Series, one of two national series that tour today's dirt tracks, will be the focus.

NATIONAL DIRT RACING ASSOCIATION

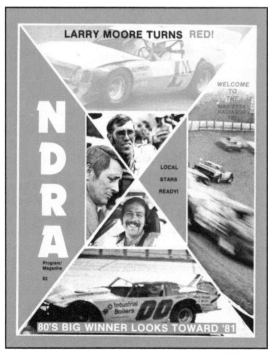

An NDRA program from 1981. (provided by Charles Hughes)

Robert Smawley started the National Dirt Racing Association (NDRA) in 1978. Smawley billed his series as, "The greatest show in dirt racing." At the time, this billing fit his series in a number of ways. Robert was able to secure big time companies like, Strohs Brewery Company, Carrera Shocks, Hoosier Racing Tires, Weber Performance Products, Consolidated Cigar Corporation, and the Dodge Corporation as some of the major sponsors for his series. He offered, unheard of at the time, high paying purses; as much as $10,000 for winning a single 100 lap race on the tour. Finally, Smawley was a keen businessman and a great showman. In the first couple of seasons, Robert convinced dirt track owners and drivers from all over the country to join his NDRA tour. So, beginning with his inaugural race on; August 5, 1978 at East Alabama Motor Speedway in Phenix City, Alabama, won by Bobby Thomas; to the series' final race on November 16, 1985 at Tri-County Motor Speedway in Hudson, North Carolina, with Kenny Brightbill taking the victory; it truly was the greatest show that late model dirt racing had ever seen.

Since the NDRA series did not begin until August of 1978; Smawley decided to carry the points championship over to the middle of 1979 to make it a full racing season. Later, in order to get the series on a seasonal racing schedule; Robert's second points championship season ran from mid-79 all the way through the '80 season. Griffin Georgia's, Leon Archer won three of the inaugural season's races, and was the NDRA's first Points Champion in '79.

In the early years of the NDRA tour; drivers and race fans from all parts of the country were learning what most people in the South already knew. The "good old boys" were hard to out run. Race fans for years had been watching Southern late model drivers like, Buck Simmons, Doug Kenimer, Charles Hughes, Bud Lunsford, Ronnie Johnson, Leon Archer, Mike Duvall, Jack Pennington, Freddy Smith, Jeff Purvis, Jack Boggs, H.E. Vineyard, C. L. Pritchett, and Bobby Thomas win races all over the South. It was no surprise, that the drivers from the South dominated the NDRA during its almost eight year run. The first season saw 10 of the 13 events captured by Southern drivers. In the second season, half of the 24 NDRA races were Southern driver victories. Finally, five of the seven NDRA Series Champions; and the driver with the most NDRA wins, Baldwin Georgia's Buck Simmons with 20 checkered flags, were all Southern dirt warriors.

The enormous success of the series was due to the promoting skills and showmanship of its founder, Robert Smawley. He was a master at getting sponsors, drivers, race fans, and race track owners on board for his, "Rock 'em, Sock 'em, Sideways Traveling Dirt Show!" This slogan was always painted on the convertible company cars he drove from one NDRA racing event to the next.

Smawley was one of the best promoters to ever be involved in late model dirt racing. In the nearby towns and cities where his events took place, he was a master at getting local businesses involved with his races. Since large crowds of race fans followed the series, Robert would point out the benefits to local businesses of sponsoring his races. For example, Marietta Radiator Shops sponsored the "Marietta Radiator 100" at West Atlanta Raceway on March 20-22, 1981. Earlier, on June 9, 1979, Looney Chevrolet in Kingsport, Tennessee, sponsored an NDRA race at Volunteer Speedway in Bull's Gap, Tennessee. Drivers and their race cars were at the Looney dealership, bringing big crowds and a lot of attention to the business. Other pioneering ideas introduced by Smawley included, perhaps the first souvenir trailers seen at dirt late model races. They also had an NDRA queen, Eva Taylor, with her famous string bikini, handing out the trophies to the winning drivers. Robert had the unique ability to build up his events; making the race fans think, "I better not miss this race because something big might happen and I want to be there to see it."

After running a few races during the first two years on Smawley's tour; Freddy Smith was the hottest driver during the 1980 NDRA season. Smith had decided to concentrate full time on winning an NDRA race. For his efforts, Freddy came away with not one win, or two wins, but five trips to victory circle in '80. What Smith did was no easy accomplishment. At the time, Rodney Combs had won, a series leading, seven races and Buck Simmons was next with six. However, that was over three seasons; All of Smith's wins came in the 1980 season, an almost unheard of feat.

Robert was also a master at getting sponsors to offer large sums of money for some of his outlandish ideas. Wins on the NDRA tour were very hard to come by. For instance in 1984, he talked Joe Lunati, of Lunati Race Cams into offering $50,000 for any driver that could win three NDRA races in a row. Smawley convinced Joe that it would be hard to win three races in a row, considering the level of competition. Well guess what? Not long after the challenge was announced, Mike Duvall, won three races in a row and took the 50 grand back to South Carolina, in August of that year. Others had done it before and after Duvall, but there was no Lunati bonus. Those included; Jeff Purvis, the final three races in '84; Buck Simmons won four in a row, in a little over two weeks (from 8- 14 to 8-22) in 1981. The last to win four in a row was Clarksville Tennessee's, Jeff Purvis in '85. Starting around 1979, Dixie Speedway had a special NDRA 100 lap race where the winner's share was raised by a $1,000 dollars every year. In 1979, Bud Lunsford won $15,000. The next year, Buck Simmons won $16,000. Some of Robert's other ideas included, large money incentives and special awards (such as free shocks, oil, fuel, and gift certificates) from sponsors for winning the pole at his events. As you can see, as long as it was the sponsors and/or the track owners money, and not his, old Smawley was just full of innovative ideas.

Smawley enjoyed the spotlight and got along with everyone around him; from the drivers; to the race fans and the track owners; and all the sponsors, everyone like Robert. All throughout the NDRA tour, there were parties (and I mean parties). Some of these parties lasted all night; with lots of alcohol, pretty girls, and some other things I won't mention here. Some of the pool parties became memorable events. They are talked about to this day by some of the drivers. For example, while racing in Tupelo, Mississippi in 1980, the tour was staying at a nearby motel; the drivers and their guests decided to ignore the pool closed sign and have an all night pool party. Well, that did not go over very well with the other guests, and especially with the motel manager. The manager had to call the police a couple of times during the night. I am sure the motel manager was overjoyed when Smawley and his NDRA tour left town. On another occasion, Rodney Combs found a lawn mower under a stairwell. It was about 4 o'clock in the morning, and Combs decided to crank the mower. He ran the lawn mower, with its loud motor running wide open for awhile. Finally, getting tired of the noise himself, he pushed the lawn mower into the motel pool. The mower ran only a few second in the water, but made some very unique noises as it "gave up the ghost." The next morning, members of the racing tour were amused at the motel employees efforts to remove the mower from the pool.

Robert enjoyed playing practical jokes on members of the tour; from the drivers, to the car owners, no one was off limits to Smawley. He enjoyed ordering wake up calls for another person's room at 4 o'clock in the morning. Other times, he would cancel someone reservations. Smawley canceled Jerry Inmon's car owner, Dick Stephens, reservation once. Stephens arrived only to find out the bad news. Later, Stephens said, "I knew it was that damn Smawley." That evening, Robert saw him at the track and roared with laughter.

There were a lot of positive changes in the world of late model dirt racing that resulted from the NDRA, and its almost eight years of existence. First, the tour brought national attention to the sport of dirt late model racing through local television, radio, and newspapers. It gave national recognition to a number of regional drivers such as, Leon Archer, Freddy Smith, Buck Simmons, Mike Duvall, Jeff Purvis, Larry Moore, Bobby Thomas, and H.E. Vineyard. The tour had a major impact on the future of racing merchandise sales, such as T-shirts, hats, jackets, and many other items. Also, a number of race related industries benefited from the NDRA. Those included; race engine companies like, Mulcuit Racing Engines, and Cornett Race Engines; racing chassis builders such as, Barry Wright, C.J. Rayburn, and WRC Chassis; racing cam companies such as Crane, and Lunati; and finally, the racing shock industry which included, Carrera, PRO, Penske, and Bilstein.

Unfortunately, it took the tragic death of NDRA star Jim Dunn, at a race Paducah, KY on May 8, 1983, to bring attention to racing safety. Dunn's death in a fiery racing accident led Robert Smawley, president of the NDRA, to lead an effort to improve the safety of race cars. This included; banning electrical fuel pumps in race cars; the standardization of fuel cells; and convincing track owners to implement a standard weight rule for race cars.

However, the NDRA was not without its negative influences to late model dirt racing. It created unfair monopolies on such thing as racing tires, Hoosier being the sole supplier of tires for the series. The tour introduced the wedge race car and the factory racing chassis, making the "home built" racing chassis obsolete. The cost of building and maintaining a race car increased, putting a lot of local race teams out of racing.

During its time, the NDRA was probably the most competitive era in late model dirt racing. The series drivers seemed to dominate in streaks. Beginning with Griffin Georgia's Leon Archer, and his rise to the top during '78 and '79. Then came Freddy Smith's run of victories in '80, winning five races. However, it was Larry Moore who won the points trophy that year. Next came Buck Simmons' dream season of '81; winning eleven races all over the country; from the Seacoast Speedway in Georgetown, Delaware; to Tuscumbia Alabama's North Alabama Speedway. Then it was the "Flintstone Flyer," Mike Duvall's turn to bring the Championship trophy home to South Carolina in '82. In '83 Rodney Combs showed that consistency does pay off by winning the NDRA Championship, despite taking only one checkered flag that year. The final two years saw Clarksville Tennessee's Jeff Purvis take his Phoenix Construction Company dirt late model on a destruction tour of the series; winning 10 of his 12 victories over the final two seasons including the point titles in '84 and '85.

Finally, Baldwin Georgia's Buck Simmons won the most races on late model dirt racing's first national tour, winning 20 races. Dayton Ohio's hard charging Larry Moore was second, with 18 wins. He was followed by Tri-City Aluminum driver, Rodney Combs with 15 trips to victory lane. South Carolina's Mike Duvall had 14 wins on the tour. Finally, Jeff Purvis rounded out the NDRA's top five in wins, with 12 checkered flags.

Buck Simmons got the NDRA's final big payday in the Fall of 1985; winning the Strohs Invitational 100 lap event at Kingsport, Tennessee along with its $30,000, and a big trophy.

Unfortunately, the National Dirt Racing Association ended after the '85 season. Also of note, NDRA star Jeff Purvis never received the money he was due for winning the final points title in 1985. All this was due in large part to Robert Smawley's mishandling of the money big time sponsors had entrusted him with. The man who was liked by all, was the victim of his own bad habits. Those habits have been well documented through the years so we will leave it there. One only wonders where late model dirt racing would be today if the NDRA had been operated in a more professional way. The world was at Robert's door. He had big name sponsors; the best drivers in the sport at the time; the national support of track owners; and publicity on the national level. All Smawley had to do was "wake up" and hear the knock at the door. Sadly, for all the drivers and race fans of the NDRA he never did.

The tenth anniversary program of the Hav-A-Tampa Dirt Racing Series. (provided by Debra Swims)

HAV-A-TAMPA DIRT RACING SERIES (UDTRA) (Xtreme)

From its first race at Lancaster (SC) Motor Speedway on May 3, 1990, as the Hav-A-Tampa Dirt Racing Series; until its last race at the Knoxville (Iowa) Raceway on October 16, 2004, as the Xtreme Dirt Racing Series; it will always be remembered as the Hav-A-Tampa Series. It was the brain child of two devoted men to the sport of late model dirt racing, Jimmy Mosteller and Mike Swims.

After the sudden end to Robert Smawley's National Dirt Racing Association at the end of the 1985 racing season, late model dirt racing had, for the most part, gone back to being a regional sport. Several years had gone by since the NDRA days and dirt racing was once again falling behind other types of motorsports racing in the country. It was like dirt racing had been all but forgotten on the national scene. Bill France's ability to secure national sponsors for his NASCAR Cup racing circuit had trickled down to a number of asphalt racing series such as, ARCA, ASA, and the other divisions in NASCAR.

Swims and Mosteller saw that poor promotion on the national level was dirt racing's biggest problem. Legendary race announcer Jimmy Mosteller was determined to bring dirt racing back to the national spotlight. His day job as Senior Vice President of the Hav-A-Tampa Cigar Company gave him an inside track to a national sponsor. After consulting with Swims, Mosteller decided to take his sponsorship idea to W.T. Morgan,III, Executive Vice President of Hav-A-Tampa. At first, Morgan only wanted to sponsor one driver and his team. However, after much discussion, the decision was made to go national with a racing program. Swims and Mosteller knew that a racing series would get the cigar company much more national exposure than sponsoring a single race team.

Mike Swims was the one who created the Hav-A-Tampa racing program. The program targeted many of the cigar company's markets in the Southeastern part of the country. The Hav-A-Tampa late model dirt races were held in these market areas. The program required race track promoters to use Hav-A-Tampa in all their advertising, be it electronic or print. The tracks were required to place signs and banners in all areas throughout the facility, and drivers were to place decals on their race cars. Hav-A-Tampa hats were mandatory at all victory celebrations.

In order to make the series unique, it had to have an exciting ending. That ending would be what came to be known as the "Hav-A-Tampa Shootout." Not every driver could enter the event. There was a certain path to the "Shootout." All the races were qualifying races; the top five in each race, plus one track promoters choice received an invitation to the season's last event, the "Hav-A-Tampa Shootout." Mike's Dad, Mickey Swims agreed to have the race at his track, the Dixie Speedway in Woodstock, Georgia. The Hav-A-Tampa executives liked Mike's program and the series was set in motion in 1990.

The first year saw 13 races, in Georgia, Alabama, Tennessee, Mississippi, North Carolina, South Carolina, and Florida. There were 12 different winners that year, Freddy Smith was the only driver with two wins. As the series grew in race dates and race car counts, it was decided that a sanctioning body was needed to provide a set of uniform rules and maintain consistency at the tracks. B.J. Parker's Southern All-Stars Dirt Racing Series agreed to be the sanctioning body, but after just a year pulled out of the commitment.

1994 again saw the series without a sanctioning body. In 1995 Mosteller came up with a name for a sanctioning body, the United Dirt Track Racing Association (UDTRA), and Mike Swims agreed to be its president. Between '96 and '99 the series experienced its biggest growth. For example, in 1999 the series had grown to 39 events, some were big two day events. They were held at places like Knoxville Tennessee's, Atomic Speedway; Route 66 Speedway in Joliet, Illinois; and Muskogee Motor Speedway in Muskogee, Oklahoma. The series continued to add new states and new race fans to its ever growing schedule. Places like, Batesville (ARK) Speedway, LaSalle (ILL) Speedway, West Plains (MO) Motor Speedway, and Davenport (Iowa) Speedway were included.

The goal of Mosteller's Hav-A-Tampa Series was two fold in the beginning. First, to have a top notch late model dirt racing series; and secondly, the image of dirt racing had to be changed in the public eye. In part because of the negative image left by Smawley's NDRA series. Mosteller had to demonstrate that his series was professionally run, and at the same time financially sound. It was certainly financially sound, with $3,000,000 in purses and a national television audience with the Speedvision network. Finally, the series staff members, track promoters, and the drivers were starting to put their best faces on in a professional manner.

2000 saw the series continue its rapid growth, with a series high 45 events, even venturing into Texas, Wisconsin, and South Dakota. However, 2000 would prove to be the last year of Hav-A-Tampa's involvement with the series. This had been expected since a corporate buyout had been developing since around 1997.

In 2001 it became the United Dirt Track Racing Association (UDTRA) Pro DirtCar Series. Mike Swims remained the dirt racing series' president and the search was on for a new corporate sponsor. After running the series for the '01 and '02 seasons the series was sold to Short Track Entertainment's Doug Bland. His company had been the UDTRA's sponsorship representative before he purchased the racing series. Doug renamed the series Xtreme DirtCar Series. After purchasing UDTRA Bland said, "This is by far the most entertaining form of motorsports out there. There is no follow the leader 400 lap stuff. There is three wide crazy action the whole time."

Doug Bland's Xtreme DirtCar Series ran the '03 season using basically the same format as the earlier UDTRA series. At the beginning of '04 Xtreme picked up a new corporate sponsor, Stacker2. The series was renamed Stacker2 Xtreme DirtCar Series. The series also picked up the Goodyear Tire and Rubber Company, which became the series' sole racing tire provider. However, Bland sold the racing series to the World of Outlaws at the end of 2004.

At the end of '04, the Lucas Oil Company bought the North American Racing Association series and renamed it, the Lucas Oil Late Model Dirt Series. The newly formed series then hired former UDTRA President, Mike Swims as part of its new management team. Swims brought his 25 years of racing experience to the new Lucas Oil series, helping develop the series' race format. Mike Swims held this position until his unfortunate death in September of 2007.

Hav-A-Tampa (Xtreme) Points Champions

1993- Clint Smith, Griffin, Ga.
1994- Scott Bloomquist, Mooresburg, Tn.
1995- Scott Bloomquist, Mooresburg, Tn.
1996- Freddy Smith, Knoxville, Tn.
1997- Billy Moyer, Batesville, Ark.
1998- Scott Bloomquist, Mooresburg, Tn.
1999- Dale McDowell, Rossville, Ga.
2000- Scott Bloomquist, Mooresburg, Tn.
2001- Rick Eckert, York, Pa.
2002- Rick Eckert, York, Pa.
2003- Scott Bloomquist, Mooresburg, Tn.
2004- Earl Pearson, Jr., Jacksonville, Fla.

Hav-A-Tampa (Xtreme) All Time Winners Top 10

1- Scott Bloomquist- Mooresburg, Tn. (100)
2- Dale McDowell, Rossville, Ga. (31)
3- Billy Moyer, Batesville, Ark. (30)
4- Wendell Wallace, Batesville, Ark. (26)
5- Freddy Smith, Knoxville, Tn. (19)
6- Ronnie Johnson, Chattanooga, Tn. (19)
7- Rick Eckert, York, Pa. (18)
8- Steve Frances, Ashland, Ky. (15)
9- Skip Arp, Georgetown, Tn. (14)
10- Dan Schlieper, Pewaukee, Wis. (13)
Jimmy Mars, Elk Mound, Wis. (13)

SOUTHERN ALL-STARS RACING SERIES

The Southern All Stars Racing Series logo.

B.J. Parker has been involved with racing in about every way imaginable throughout his life. In his younger days he was a driver, and a pretty good one although he would never admit it. Later, he owned Sayre (ALA) Speedway for a brief time in 1975. He then promoted races, first at the Dixie Speedway in Midfield, Alabama; and in the late 70's, at the Birmingham International Raceway in Birmingham, Alabama. At the height of his promotional career B.J. promoted as many as 100 races a year all over the Southeast.

Parker has always had a love for dirt racing, and in 1983 he founded the Southern All-Stars Racing Series.

Parker started the series for the local drivers, he said, "The drivers with a lot of talent, but not a lot of financial backing." In the beginning, he actually rented race tracks and promoted his races, using the track's own staff to help run the events. He would invite the best drivers from five or six different tracks to come and race in his series for an advertised purse. "This," he said, "was why I named it the Southern All Stars."

During the first couple of years, Parker would actually lose money on some races. However, B.J. always paid the advertised purse no matter if he made a profit or not. Parker once said, "Some nights the crowds were so small, instead of introducing the drivers to the crowd, I thought about introducing the crowd to the drivers."

Parker was instrumental in the success of the series from the start. In the early days, most racing deals with track owners were done with a hand shake. He proved to be a man of his word; as mentioned, he always paid his advertised purses; he treated every driver the same; he set the rules and never deviated from them. He was one of the few promoters who knew the drivers side of the racing business as well as the promotional side.

All the drivers in his series liked B.J. Parker because he was a stern, but at the same time, a fair man. Four time series points winner and current World of Outlaws late model driver, Clint Smith credits Parker for jump starting his racing career. In 1999, Lynn Acklin became General Manager of the series, as Parker scaled back his traveling. Acklin had started working with B.J. on his asphalt series. Through the years the SAS has operated in conjunction with several major corporate sponsors including, Busch Beer and the O'Reilly's Auto Parts banners.

In the SAS's first year, the series ran a total of 13 races in, Georgia, Tennessee, Alabama, And Mississippi. The series' first race was held on March 19, 1983 at the Gulf Coast Checkered Flag Speedway in Biloxi Mississippi. The driver who won that race, along with the most wins that season was Angie Louisiana's Chick Boyd with three checkered flags. The first ASA series point champion was Tupelo, Mississippi's Don Hester.

After 31 years, Parker sold the Southern All-Stars Racing Series to Charles Roberts and David Miller in 2004. During their eight year run, the series experienced some up and down times. It seemed as the country's economy went so did the series. After having received several offers to buy the SAS over the years, Roberts decided to sell the series to Huntsville Alabama Native Matt Wagner in early 2012.

Wagner kept long time series General Manager Lynn Acklin to continue to oversee the operation. Wagner bought the SAS series with the idea of bringing it back to its home state of Alabama. Also, he wanted to, in his own words, "rebuild the series." He Wanted to have more local late model driver participation. His objective was to lower the racing purses and thus have less big name stars. He also lowered ticket prices for the SAS events. Wagner felt that with these two changes he would have bigger car counts and more race fans in attendance.

During its long running history the series has crowned a lot of series point champions. They include, the series' only four time champion, Senoia, Georgia's Clint Smith and three time winner Crossville, Tennessee's Randy "Dream" Weaver. Two time winners are, Ronnie Johnson, Chris Madden, Roger Best, Rex Richey, Ivedent Loyd Jr., and Riley Hickman the 2014 SAS points champion. The top three in all time wins are, Chattanooga Tennessee's Ronnie Johnson with 62 victories, followed by Gray Court South Carolina's Chris Madden with 44, and Dale McDowell of Rossville, Georgia with 40 victory lane appearances (at the start of 2014).

The nation's longest running dirt late model touring series continues to give, both drivers and race fans alike, a quality racing program at reasonable price. This is just how the legendary racing pioneer, B.J. Parker envisioned his SAS series from the beginning. Sadly, B.J. Parker passed away in April of 2011. The always smiling Parker will be missed in the racing community.

LUCAS OIL LATE MODEL DIRT SERIES

The Lucas Oil Late Model Dirt Series logo.

In 2004 the Lucas Oil Company acquired the Lexington, Kentucky based North American Racing Association (NARA). The NARA had just signed Lucas Oil to be their corporate sponsor for the 2005 season. However, with Lucas' purchase of NARA, it will now be under the direction of I-10 Promotions, and the series name will be changed to the "Lucas Oil Late Model Dirt Series."

Bob Patison, Executive Vice President of Lucas Oil, said the reason behind the companies purchase was all about building a professional national late model dirt racing series. Patison wanted to use the series to market the companies' product lines and to ultimately build a strong television package to help lure additional sponsors to the series, and to the many race teams that compete in the series.

The series, under the name NARA DirtCar Series completed a short eight race tour in 2004, with Moweaqua Illinois' Shannon Babb winning the series' first recognized point title. During the off season and into early '05 the series now known by its familiar name, Lucas Oil Late Model Dirt Series, swelled to 30+ events for the coming '05 season. In addition, more money came to the series in the form of several new incentives. Perhaps the biggest was what came to be known as "The Winner's Circle Plan." This plan rewarded the top 10 in points with a $500 per finishing position at each race in a 30 race schedule for a $150,000 increase in prize money. Also, the points champion at the end of the year will receive $30,000, with 10th place paying an amazing $10,000.

Also, 2005 saw Lucas Oil Owner, Forrest Lucas, and V.P. Bob Patison bring in the former UDTRA/Hav-A-Tampa president, Mike Swims to assist with the planning and development of the series. In addition to Swims, the series continued the relationship with a number of employees. Spencer Wilson would be the Race Director (he was replaced in '07 by another UDTRA/Hav-A-Tampa employee, Richie Lewis); Rick Schwallie would become Assistant Series Director and Photographer; Cole Lewis, Events Coordinator; finally, James Essex would be the voice of the Lucas Oil Series as the announcer.

To show the company's commitment to late model dirt racing was going to be a long term association, the company purchased the Wheatland (MO) Raceway. Lucas renamed the speedway, the Lucas Oil Speedway. The track has seen extensive renovations and updates and is now one of the premiere dirt tracks in the country. The Speedway hosts a number of special events; like the annual Show-Me 100 and its big $30,000 pay check; and the CMH Diamond Nationals with the winner receiving a diamond ring in addition to a $10,000 payday.

There have now been over 400 races since the series began. Martinville Indiana's Don O'Neal won the first race under the Lucas Oil Late Model Dirt Series name on February 7, 2005, at Gibsonton, Florida's East Bay Raceway. As of the end of 2014, there have been 63 different winners; 2150 super late model drivers have competed in the series; and the contest for the driver with the most wins (at the start of 2015) is a neck and neck battle between, Scott Bloomquist with 53 Checkered flags and Jimmy Owens with 52 series wins.

There have been only five Lucas Oil Late Model Dirt Series Champions since 2004. Shannon Babb won the first under the NARA in '04. Jacksonville Florida's Earl Pearson Jr. won the next four, '05, '06, '07, and '08; followed by Mooresburg, Tennessee racing legend Scott Bloomquist in '09, and '10. The next three were won by the "Newport Nightmare," Jimmy Owens in '11, '12, and '13. In 2014, the current and defending champion is Martinsville, Indiana's Don O'Neal. The series is televised by MAVTV on the Lucas Dirt TV schedule, with Bob Dillner, involved with the broadcasting of the racing series' events.

2015 is looking like it is going to be one of the best years yet for the Lucas Oil Late model Dirt Series. The series has lined up a 50 race schedule for the year. The current top five in points through the June 13th "Clash at the Mag" were: Jonathan Davenport, Earl Pearson Jr., Jimmy Owens, defending Champion Don O' Neal, and Scott Bloomquist. The driver with the most wins so far is, Mount Airy North Carolina's, Jonathan Davenport with five victory lane celebrations. Look for more exciting racing in 2015. As baseball great Yogi Berra once said, "It ain't over til it's over."

CHAPTER FOUR:
SOUTHERN DIRT TRACKS PAST AND PRESENT

It's time to have a historic look at some of the finest dirt tracks in the nation and as you the race fan will see they all have a historical past with late model dirt racing. Most have a unique history that you will find very fascinating. First we look at two tracks, that sadly, are no longer with us, but played an important role in dirt racing history. The first we have already mentioned, the "one mile dirt oval" known as Lakewood Speedway that was located in South Atlanta. Next, we take a look at the famed Atomic Speedway that was located off I-40 near Knoxville, Tennessee. Finally, we look at a number of tracks throughout the South that are making, or in some cases, have already made their own dirt racing history.

LAKEWOOD SPEEDWAY

A view from the air of the famed Lakewood Speedway, Located in Atlanta, GA. (Photo courtesy of Leon Sells)

Most of the early auto racing history at Lakewood was covered in chapter one. So let's take a look at Lakewood Speedway after World War II. In 1946 as racing resumed at Lakewood, several organizations (AAA, USAC, and IMCA) held a number of races at the track. In addition, Lakewood became the premier track for the National Stock Car Racing Association.

After NSCRA folded, Bill France's NASCAR held their first race at the track in 1951. NASCAR would go on to hold eleven Grand National (now called Sprint Cup Series) events and two convertible division races during the 50's. It was NASCAR that put Lakewood back on the map. This was an ideal partnership for both NASCAR and Lakewood Speedway. At the time, it was one of NASCAR's largest race tracks. It was also a central location for a sport that was largely a Southern sport at the time.

After Atlanta International Raceway opened in 1960 Lakewood lost its NASCAR races and fell on hard times. However, in 1962 a group of promoters, and drivers, Alf Knight, Ernie Moore, Jim Summerour, and the legendary race announcer Jimmy Mosteller, pooled a large sum of money to upgrade and improve the safety of the speedway. During the 60's and into the early 70's Lakewood held a number of late model dirt races. These races drew large crowds and things were looking up for the grand old speedway. Among the late model race winners were Dan Lingerfelt, Leon Sells, Charlie Mincey; and two racing legends, Curtis Turner and Buck Simmons, also won a number of races.

During the mid-70's Lakewood again fell on hard times. This was due to a number of new dirt tracks opening in the metro Atlanta area. Chief among them were, Dixie Speedway, Rome Speedway, and West Atlanta Raceway. As Charlie Mincey won the last race of 1978, track promoters noticed the declining attendance and dwindling profits. The final two late model races ever held at the historic track were in 1979. Dan Lingerfelt won the next to last race, driving for George Elliott (Bill Elliott's father). The final race was held on Labor Day September 3, 1979. It could have been a Hollywood script as one of the track's all time winners, the legendary Buck Simmons won the final race at the grand old speedway.

ATOMIC SPEEDWAY

A cross track view of the main grandstands at the legendary Atomic Speedway.(Photo courtesy of Nick Nicholson)

I was traveling West on I-40 out of Knoxville the other day and happened to look over where Atomic Speedway once stood. Somehow, in my mind, I was hoping to see the giant wooden race car, perhaps even the red clay of the track and the old grandstands, or just maybe the old blue and red scoring tower with the big Pepsi logos. All those reminders of "the world's fastest 1/3 mile dirt track" are now gone. Time and property values may have taken away the famed Atomic Speedway, but one thing is certain no one can take away those 36 years of memories the track left the race fans and those drivers who drove her historic high banks.

Atomic Speedway opened in 1970, the brain child of owner-builder Bob Martin. Bob wanted to open a top notch dirt racing facility in East Tennessee that would be both, race fan friendly and a race driver's dream to compete on. In both areas Bob Martin came out a winner.

The speedway was located off I-40 near the Roane-Loudon county lines. At the track's opening it had the widest racing surface of any track in the area. The track was very fan friendly, with seating very close to the track. I remember the first time I sat in the stands for one of those famous 100 lap events. After the race, my wife and I stopped by a McDonalds on the way home. I noticed the other customers in line were staring wide-eyed at me. I had to go to the bathroom, so I happened to look in the mirror and saw what the other customers had been staring at. I thought I had changed colors, my face and arms were black with tire rubber and dust. Any race fan who has sat in the stands at Atomic knows exactly what I am referring to.

Powell Tennessee's Buddy Weaver won the first feature race at Atomic before almost 400 race fans. I once told someone, "I don't care how many races you win at Atomic, no one can do what Buddy Weaver did. He won the first race." Martin continued to make improvement to both, the track and the other speedway facilities for the race fans and drivers throughout his ownership.

In the late 70's Martin sold the track to Bill, Jack, and Jim Ogle. The new owners made more improvements to the facility. They added the famous blue and red air-conditioned V.I.P. Tower and increased the banking of the race track. Also, the old guardrail was replaced with a concrete wall for driver safety. The added banking increased race speeds dramatically. Herman Goddard cracked the 13-second barrier in 1973, with a lap of 13.75. Larry Moore lowered the mark in 1979 with a lap of 12.93.

The track surface was reworked in the mid-80's, resulting in the first 11-second lap being turned in 1986. My dad and I were at Atomic in the Spring of 1986. The area had experienced rain all week and the track's surface was "sticking like glue." That night three cars broke the World qualifying record for a one-third mile dirt track. The first was Gary Hall, next was H.E. Vineyard, followed by Scott Bloomquist who set the final mark of 11.29 in the Katch One #18 race car. Scott later broke that record in 1991 with a lap of 10.75. A record that still stands today.

Stuart Randolph bought the race track in 1994, owning it for only a year. In 1996 Carson Branum purchased the speedway. The race track continued to see a host of changes. The concourse was paved and a new entrance was added, along with a new pit entrance. In 1997 the pits were moved entirely outside the track, giving the race fans a better view of the racing activities. The name of the track was changed to a more modern sounding, Atomic Motor Speedway. The year 2002 saw the new Musco lighting system installed, along with a modern scoreboard.

Jim Varnell, a Knoxville businessman, bought the track in 2002. Under Varnell's watch new improvements in the infield concession facilities and new restrooms were added. After a continued decrease in race fans and race car counts Varnell sold the track to Lenoir City's Ed Adams in 2005. Adams planned to improve the lighting in the pits and repaint the entire facility. However, in 2006 the unthinkable was about to happen. The Roane County Commission approved rezoning of the 28-acre site, from commercial to industrial. This paved the way for Ed Adams to sell the property to Nebraska's Crete Carrier Corporation for a trucking terminal. The Last race was held on November 4, 2006.

During her time, Atomic Speedway was the proving ground for many of the area's top late model drivers like, Tootle Estes, Herman Goddard, Scott Bloomquist, H.E. Vineyard, Ken Phillips, Ronnie Johnson, Skip Arp, Billy Ogle Jr., and many others. Johnny Gibson was the first late model track champion in 1970, and David Crabtree was the last in 2006. During her 36 years, Billy Ogle Jr. won the most late model Championships at eight; while Ken Phillips, Tootle Estes, Jack Trammell, and H.E. Vineyard had three titles each.

Atomic played host to a number of classic races over her 36 years. Those races included, The Hall of Fame 100, The Cabin Fever 100, and The Tennessee State Dirt Championships, all were annual events. In addition, many national and regional touring series such as, NDRA, Southern All-Stars, Hav-A-Tampa, S.T.A.R.S., World of Outlaws Late Model Dirt Series, and many others held races at Atomic. The famed Atomic Speedway may be gone, but as sure as the Sun comes up tomorrow, she will continue to live on in our hearts.

SMOKY MOUNTAIN SPEEDWAY

The stands and press box at Smoky Mountain Speedway. (Photo by the author)

Smoky Mountain Speedway has a historical past that might rival that of the Eldora Speedway, and its classic World 100; or the famed Pennsboro Speedway, where the "wedge" late models of the early 80's were introduced. "The Mountain," as she is know by race fans and drivers alike; was opened as Smoky Mountain Raceway by Earl Orr in 1964, and 51 years later it is still writing a chapter in East Tennessee racing history.

Smoky Mountain Speedway was originally about the size of Bristol, Tennessee's NASCAR track. The track's size (a ½ mile when first built) soon caught the eye of Bill France and NASCAR. Smoky Mountain secured a NASCAR Grand National event (now Sprint Cup) in 1965, with Dick Hutcherson winning the first NASCAR race at the speedway. The track hosted a total of 12 Grand National races between 1965 and the early 70's. Cup drivers who raced at Smoky Mountain included, Bobby and Donnie Allison, David Pearson, Buddy Baker, Richard Petty, Bobby Isaac, Dave Marcis, and NASCAR's first African-American driver

Wendell Scott. In 1968 the track was paved in an effort to keep its NASCAR races.

During the track's heyday in the late 60's, Don Naman was the promoter and General Manager of the track. Naman had a very successful record at other racing facilities before taking the reins at Smoky Mountain. NASCAR was looking to add another super-speedway to its tour. Naman tried to convince Bill France that the Knoxville area would be the perfect location for the track. However, Knoxville and Knox County leaders were against the idea, saying they did not want "the type of crowds" that those events drew. The end result was, the area lost its opportunity for a su-perspeedway and France built the 2.66 mile track in Talladega, Alabama. Two other major losses followed. France hired Naman away from Smoky Mountain to be the General Manager of the new Talladega track and NASCAR trimmed its schedule from over 50 events down to 30 a year. Smoky Mountain was dropped from the schedule and the Bristol Raceway kept its racing events.

After the departure of NASCAR in 1972, the track continued to maintain some levels of success. The Orr family had already sold

A view from atop the retaining wall looking up the front straight-away at Smoky Mountain. (Photo provided by the author)

the track to a group from North Carolina. Local drivers like Tootle Estes, J.T. Kerr, Jim Hunter, L.D. Ottinger, and others raced the weekly program at the track. The track also hosted a number of special races that attracted the likes of Jack Ingram, and the legendary "Alabama Gang" member Red Farmer.

The decline of asphalt racing almost spelled the doom for Smoky Mountain Speedway in the mid-70's. Competition from area dirt tracks, like Atomic Speedway, caused the track to see a downturn in fan attendance and race car counts. The owner's of Corbin Speedway purchased the track with the intent of putting a dirt track inside the existing paved track. The track closed in 1977 after that idea failed to materialize.

Bill, Jim, and Jack Ogle (the owners of Atomic at the time) saved the doomed speedway by tearing up the asphalt and reopening it as a dirt track in 1979. The track had and up and down success on the dirt racing scene under the Ogles ownership. Racing Programs alternated between Friday and Saturday nights during the Ogle years. The track's up and down support could not be blamed on the lack of quality racing events. Smoky Mountain hosted several NDRA races during the early to mid-80's. A $250,000 NDRA purse was on the track's schedule for September of 1984, with $20,000 going to the winner. Jeff Purvis, Billy Moyer, Buck Simmons, and most of the NDRA regulars, along with about 200 other drivers showed up for the event. Tom Helfrich won the race, taking home one of the biggest paydays in the history of the track.

The Ogles sold the speedway in the mid-80's, This started a period of rapid ownership turnaround. In the late 80's until the early 90's a number of owners tried a number of different ideas to improve fan attendance and car counts. Among the many ideas tried were; running a Friday Night program to avoid competition from other area tracks; and changing the name to Smoky Mountain Speedway. Finally, the race track was reduced in size, from a ½ mile to its present 4/10 mile. One of the reasons for this was to lessen the wear on the race engines of the drivers.

The mid-90's saw a period of some success under the ownership of Fred Houser, Billy Loope, Ken Cooke, and Charlie Hill.

The owners changed some of the racing divisions in their race program. This, along with the addition of a number of touring series programs, such as the Hav-A-Tampa and the Southern All-Stars appeared to put life back into the track.

In the late 90's Jim Varnell purchased the track. Jim wanted to get away from the "open engines" and the high costs of the super late models. He introduced the "limited" late model program to Smoky Mountain Speedway. This program used the cost efficient "steel head" engines and made racing more affordable for the local race teams. The result was an increase in fan attendance and race car counts of upwards of 30 cars for this new program.

Varnell sold the track to one of the former owners, Fred Houser. He continued to use Varnell's racing program and the car counts rose to over 100 race cars each week. Houser added a few special races and the track appeared to finally be on the right course. In 1999 Atomic Speedway owner Carson Branum bought the track from Varnell, who was in bad health at the time. Branum also owned Crossville Raceway at the time, and just a year and a half after buying it closed Smoky Mountain. Many in the racing circles still wonder if Branum bought the track with this idea in mind. After closing the track in the Summer of 2000 Branum cited environmental concerns and complaints from area residents as the reasons for the closure.

Smoky Mountain remained closed for two years. Branum suffered a series of financial set backs and lost both Smoky Mountain and Crossville and was forced to sell Atomic at the end of 2002. Fred Houser held a note on Smoky Mountain Speedway's property, and not wanting to run the track put it on the auction block in January 2003. Maryville businessmen Denny and Bill Garner bought the track. Smoky Mountain had been closed for over 2 years and needed a lot of repairs. However, by April of 2003 the track was reopened and the fans flocked to the track although race car counts were modest at best.

An accident involving late model drivers, Todd Hunt and Tommy Kerr, proved to be the undoing for the Garners in 2004. After Hunt's car was hit by the Kerr car, Todd Hunt's car erupted into flames and he narrowly missed being severely burned. The track only had a water truck for fire protection, it proved no match for the high octane racing fuel. Fans and race drivers questioned the Garner brothers dedication to driver protection. The Garners tried to assure the fans and drivers of their commitment to driver safety by signing a deal with a neighboring county's rescue squad. Race fans and drivers started staying away form the track and criticism of the Garners continued to grow week after week. Despite bringing in a number of touring series such as, the national World of Outlaws Late Model Dirt Series and the regional Southern All-Stars the Garners could never over come the unfortunate turn of events. The 2004 and 2005 racing seasons saw attendance and car counts in a steady decline and at the end of the 2005 racing season the track closed and was put up for sale.

After the track closed in 2005, the 44 acre site was being considered for a new county fairgrounds site. During the time it was in the hands of the Blount County Fairground Commission. It was during the Winter of 2006 that Kevin Coffey came to the rescue of Smoky Mountain Speedway. Through Kevin's hard work and several meetings with the Blount County Commissioners he was able to get a 21 to 21 vote to purchase the speedway. Work began in early 2007 on the race track, which had sat idle for almost two years. The speedway had to have extensive work done to all areas of the facility. Kevin and his wife, father, other family members, and even Kevin's CDE Electrical Contracting employees began repairs to the buildings, grandstands, and pit areas (an outside pit). They even added a new lighting system in the process.. According to Kevin, the total spent was well over $250,000.

Through Kevin's dedication and hard work the track was able to open for the 2007 racing season, with Brady Albright managing the track that year. The racing program included, super late models, steel head late models and a few other divisions of race cars. In addition, some special racing events were held. However, 2008 saw a downturn in the economy and the track started to suffer. In 2009 Coffey was looking for some partnership in the track to keep racing alive at Smoky Mountain. Three area businessmen would join Kevin in the in the racing venture, Stanley Best, Roger Sellers, and Larry Garner. This eventually resulted in what is today a four way partnership in Smokey Mountain Speedway. It has turned into a family business for the partners, with family members from all sides working at the track.

The years from about 2010 to the present have seen the track use a number of racing programs, from bi-weekly to monthly racing shows. During 2014 and into 2015 the track ran a lot of high profile, high paying touring events to the delight of race fans from all over the region. These include a number of regional series such as, the Southern All-Stars Dirt Racing Series, Ultimate Super Late Model Series, the Old Man's Garage Spring Nationals; and the two national series, the Lucus Oil Late Model Dirt Series, and the World of Outlaws Late Model Series.

Smoky Mountain Speedway has a lengthy past in Southern dirt racing history. Hopefully, she will continue to write that history long into the future.

TAZEWELL SPEEDWAY

View of victory lane at the Tazewell Speedway. (Photo provided by the author)

Since Blaine and Bill Frazier built and opened Tazewell Speedway in June 1965, two things have become the speedway's trademarks. The first are the loyal fans, many have been coming to the track since that first June race. Week after week race fans fill the stands, especially when the super late models race at the speedway. The final trademark was added in 1982, the blistering lap speeds turned since Blaine added the high banking to the track.

It all started after Blaine and some others watched a race at the 3/8 mile red clay race track known as 411 Speedway in Seymour, Tennessee. Blaine and Bill decided on a section of their father's farmland to build the race track. Without their fathers permission they called Lawrence Hurst, who was in the construction business, and invited him to start shaping the race track with his dozing equipment. At first the track was almost flat, with little banking in the turns or on the straightaways. Blaine recently told me he had two classes of race cars at first. He said those were, a "sportsman" class (flat heads/6 cylinders) and the "jalopy" class (fenderless race cars). Frazier said some of the first year drivers included, Buddy Rogers, Windy York, "Lil" Bill Corum, and "Pig" Wilson.

Around 1982 Bill and Blaine ended their partnership in the track, with Blaine becoming sole owner of the race track. 1982 also saw the change that made the track what it is known as today, a high banked 1/3 mile red clay oval. In addition to adding the high banks to the track, Blaine continued to make changes to other areas of the facility, adding new seats, concessions, and bathrooms. Also, the race track's wooden walls were changed to guard railing.

The Track was closed in 1985 and remained closed until 1990. Then, according to Blaine, David Pierce leased the speedway for a short stint that lasted about a year. Later, Blaine Frazier returned and kept the track until he sold it to John and Lori Thompson around the end of 1995. John had wanted to own a race track for some time. It was while competing as a driver that he saw the great potential of Blaine's Tazewell Speedway. John was also the one who had Harriman Tennessee's James Vanover and his concrete finishing company install the concrete walls around the track.

During John's ownership, he raced at Tazewell and, as the new owner, wanted to take the track to the next level. He wanted to secure the track a race date with the new touring series, the Hav-A-Tampa Dirt Racing Series. John Thompson got his wish. Another track failed to get their race date with the series and Tazewell was given the race. According to some, the race was one of the best ever run at Tazewell Speedway. This was the turning point that launched the little speedway onto the national scene. Speedvision TV would broadcast Tazewell's Hav-A-Tampa races for the next two years and race fans all across the country would know about the fast Taz.

According to Blaine, Thompson sold the track to Bill Webb around 2002, holding the loan on the Speedway himself. John took the track back around 2003 and kept the race track until 2005. That's when he sold it to former dirt late model ace, Gary Hall, the present owner. Under Gary's watch the track has continued to gain national recognition, hosting a number of regional super late model series, such as the Old Man's Garage Spring Nationals, and the Southern All Stars. Both of the dirt late model national tours, the Lucas Oil and the World of Outlaws, make regular stops at the "FastTaz," bringing some of the best super late model drivers and race fans from all over the nation. It was at one of these national events in 2012 that Scott Bloomquist set a blistering track record speed of 10.82 seconds for a single lap around the speedway's high banks.

On my trips to the Tazewell Speedway, two things are certain; you are going to see some of the best high speed racing in the country, and Gary Hall and his staff are going to make you feel just like family. The 50th anniversary year of 2015 has already seen some thrilling racing. Local driver Billy Ogle Jr. won his first World of Outlaws race in April. He made a thrilling last lap pass of super late model star Josh Richards coming off turn four on the final lap, taking Newport's Jimmy Owens with him for second place.

Tazewell Speedway has enjoyed 50 years of great racing, with some of the best drivers in the country visiting the Track. If I were a betting man I believe she is going to see a lot more great races in the coming years.

Looking toward the pits form the main grandstands at Volunteer Speedway at Bulls Gap, Tennessee. (photo courtesy of Nick Nicholson)

Perhaps no other dirt track has played such a unique role in my memories of late model dirt racing over the last fifty plus years as has the Volunteer Speedway at Bull's Gap, Tennessee. My emotional spectrum has ran its course at this high banked dirt facility.

On June 9, 1979 my happiest memory occurred, watching my longtime racing friend, H.E. Vineyard win a thrilling NDRA race at Volunteer Speedway over Buck Simmons and a star studded field of late model drivers. On August 20, 1982, I experienced the opposite end of the emotional spectrum. My saddest emotions occurred upon learning that Tootle Estes, one of my favorite drivers, had just died of a massive heart attack only a short time after I had watched him win a hard fought feature race over long time rival, "Little" Bill Corum and others in the closing laps of the race.

Hugh and Louise Goan had construction work begin on what became known as the Volunteer Speedway in 1973. Located off Interstate 81 at exit 23 in Bull's Gap, Tennessee. The 4/10th of a mile high banked clay oval opened in mid-season of 1974. The winner of the first late model race was Danny Burks out of Richlands, Virginia, driving a 1973 Chevrolet to the feature win. Ralph Moore was the track promoter during the heydays of the NDRA. Throughout the track's 41 year history some of East Tennessee's finest dirt late model drivers have scored victories at the track. Those Late model dirt warriors include, Scott Bloomquist, "Little" Bill Corum, Jimmy Owens, Herman Goddard, Tootle Estes, Billy Ogle Jr., Ronnie Johnson, H.E. Vineyard, Tommy Kerr, Buddy Rogers, Rusty Goddard, L.D. Ottinger, Vic Hill, Scott Sexton, and Gusty Christenberry to name but a few of East Tennessee's best.

Over the Years a number of regional, as well as national dirt late model touring series have done battle on the high banked of Volunteer Speedway. Those include, the first national touring series, the National Dirt Racing Association in the late 70's to the mid-80's, with Buck Simmons, Freddy Smith, and Leon Archer some of the drivers taking victories in the series. The Hav-A-Tampa series also made several trips to "The Gap" with drivers like, Marshall Green and Freddy Smith scoring wins. Currently the two national tours make regular stops at the speedway. Lucas Oil Late Model Series winner's have included, Scott Bloomquist, Dale McDowell, Billy Ogle Jr., Jimmy Owens, and Chris Madden. The World of Outlaws Dirt Late Model winner's include dirt stars like, Shane Clanton, and Jimmy Owens, who sometimes competes in both national touring series.

Today, many regional dirt racing series gladly include Volunteer Speedway on their yearly schedules. Those include the longest running regional series, the Southern All-Stars Racing Series, and others like the Ultimate Super Late Model Series and the Carolina Clash Super Late Model Series.

According to Robert Walden, long time public relations director at Volunteer, late model track championships started in 1975 and continue today. Walden said, late model track champions over the years include, Knoxville's Herman Goddard, who was the first to be crowned; Red Ledford of Morristown in 1976; Walter Ball of Johnson City, in 1977; H.E. Vineyard of Powell in 1978, '79, '81, and '84; Tootle Estes of Knoxville, in 1980; "Little" Bill Corum of

Maynardville, in 1982; Bill Morton of Church Hill, in 1983; Howard Collins of Greenville, in 1985; and J.T. Kerr of Rockford, in 1989.

Walden said the late model Champions of the '90's included; Herman Goddard of Knoxville, in 1990; Scott Sexton of pigeon Forge, in 1991 and '95; Gary Myers of Greenville, in 1992; John A. Utsman of Bluff City, in 1993; David Burks of Richland, Va., in 1994; Randy Ford of Johnson City, in 1996; Vic Hill of Morristown, in 1997 and '98; and Dale Ball of Johnson City, in 1999. Robert said, as the new century at Volunteer began, Morristown's Vic Hill captured the 2000 super late model title; Kerry Jones of Bristol, won the 2001 title; Mark Douglas won back to back title, in 2002 and '03; Rick Norris of Kingsport, won his first title in 2004. Vic Hill again won the super late model title in 2005. Rodgersville's Mike Smith won his first track championship in 2006. Bristol's Kerry Jones scored another title in 2007. Jeff Maupin of Greenville won the track title in 2008. Hill entered a class all to himself in 2009, by winning his fifth super late model title. Finally, Greenville's Jeff Maupin won his second driving title in 2010.

Beginning in 2011 late models stopped competing on a weekly basis and titles were awarded for pro (crate) late model champions. The first was Dale Ball of Johnson City, in 2011 and again in 2012. Tim Byrd of Jonesborough won the crate title in 2013. In 2014 two track titles were won; Jason Manly of Loudon, in steel head late model, and Tim Maupin, in the pro crate late model.

Speed has been the one thing that Volunteer Speedway has been known for throughout its forty plus years of history. A number of different types of race cars have set track speed records at the Gap. Those include, Gusty Christenberry's run what you brung "outlaw lexan wagon," which qualified at 11.74 seconds in 2003. Then came Terry Gray (The Bartlett Bullet) from Bartlett, Tennessee, who toured the track at an amazing lap of 11.67 seconds in a sprint car in 2008. Next was Kasey Kahne's World of Outlaws sprint car lap of 10.25 seconds in 2010. That was the fastest lap ever turned at what has became known as the "World's Fastest Dirt Track." However, Batesville, Arkansas's Wendell Wallace holds the current super late model record at 12.001 seconds set in 1998, before the track was reshaped in 1999.

Today the red clay, high banked speedway is owned by Joe and Phyllis Loven. I have enjoyed going to "The Gap" since the late 70's; and the super late model touring series schedule, along with the weekly racing programs continue to be one of the best in the South.

BOYD'S SPEEDWAY

A view of Boyd's Speedway from the air in the early 50's. Note there is no I-75 off to the right of the track. (Photo provided by Katy Boyd-Coulter)

Boyd's Speedway was the vision of E.A. Boyd, who wanted a race track closer to home so he and his friends could go and watch stock car racing. At first the track was going to be built in the Spring Creek area of East Ridge, Tennessee. However, East Ridge City officials were against the idea citing, the crowds it would draw and the noise as the reasons for not approving the Speedway. This is why the location of Boyd's Speedway is where it is today. The track is located just a few hundred feet inside Georgia at the Georgia/

Tennessee state line. Construction began on the speedway in 1951 and the first race took place on October 5, 1952.

E.A. Boyd ran the track from its opening in 1952 until 1963. Like the most of the dirt tracks at the time, Boyd's ran jalopy and sportsman classes at first, but by the end of the 50's the track was running what would become known the "late model" race cars. They included, 1955-56 Chevrolets and Fords, which would be the mainstay in late model racing well into the late 60's. Most of these cars were "home built" race cars. One of the early race car builders in the area was Tunnel Hill Georgia's legendary Bob Wright, who built a number of race cars in the 50's and 60's for such drivers as Jody Ridley, "Wild Man" Jerry Smith, Leon Brindle, Dave Wright, and Joe Lee Johnson. He became well known in the area as well as the whole region for the quality race cars he built.

Boyd had a love for all types of automobile racing, jalopies, sportsman, skeeters, you name it, he loved to watch car races. In 1957 he had the USAC midgets at Boyd's. However, the USAC race was on a Tuesday night and did not go over very well, with only a small crowd showing up for the event. However, E.A. was in the stands that night and enjoyed watching a very good midget race, his son Elmer (Butch) Boyd told me.

In 1962 the track was paved and hosted the first of two NASCAR Grand National (now Sprint Cup) events, The Confederate 200 on August 2, 1962. The race was won by "Little" Joe Weatherly, in a Bud Moore 61 Pontiac. Glenn "Fireball" Roberts finished a close second. In 1964 Otis Gaither ran the speedway for a brief stint, changing the name to, Chattanooga International Speedway. Also, the final NASCAR Grand National event was held, the Confederate 300 on June 19, 1964. This race was held during the Plymouth and Dodge "Hemi" era in NASCAR. Those cars were dominating NASCAR races at the time; and true to form this race too was won by David Pearson in a Cotton Owens 64 Dodge, with Richard Petty finishing second in a 64 Plymouth.

Jimmy Baker, former midget racer from the Atlanta area promoted Boyd's during the mid-60's. The track was very successful under Baker's management. Some of the best Late model drivers to ever race Boyd's Speedway came during the mid-60's to the early 70's. Those drivers included, Jody Ridley, Friday Hassler, Bob Burcham, Algie Robinson, Bobby Fryar, Snooks Defore, Fred Cook, and Harold Fryar to name but a few.

Katy Coulter, E.A. Boyd's Daughter, told me an interesting story about the track's famous chicken sandwiches during the time Baker promoted the speedway. She told me that Jimmy was friends with S. Truett Cathy, founder of Chick-fil-A. Katy said Baker got the recipe for the chicken sandwiches from Cathy, along with the type of deep fryer to use to fry them. She said Baker served those Boyd's chicken sandwiches at the speedway the whole time he was there. When she said that, I remembered how good they were. My dad and I would always eat 2 or 3 every time we went to Boyd's to watch a race. Also, I remember the officials at the gate would let people in just long enough to buy the chicken sandwiches to take home by the sackfuls.

Two local contractors, Bobby Bailey and Fred Frost, had a short stint at running the speedway at the beginning of the 70's. Later, Elmer (Butch) Boyd took over the operations at his father's famed speedway in 1971. He made several upgrades to the speedway. The major change involved taking the old retaining walls down and replacing it with guard rails. Elmer ran several classes of race cars, including the very popular 9 to 1 class in which Jody Ridley and his 64 Falcon were frequent winners. Some of the drivers in this popular class included, Leon Sells, Billy McGinnis, and Bob Burcham. Boyd closed the track at the end of the 1973 season and the speedway remained closed until 1975. However, a couple of Shrine 100 lap races were held around 1974, that brought in such drivers as the "Bayou Bandit" Freddy Fryar, Jody Ridley, and even country music's Marty Robbins in a Double Cola sponsored race car.

In 1975 Chatsworth Georgia's Keith Tenney, owner of Tenney Construction Company bought the track. He tore up the asphalt at the end of 1976 and Boyd's Speedway was once again a dirt track. However, Keith's ownership was short lived and E.A. Boyd's wife, Mollie, took ownership of the track and it was closed between 1979 and 1982.

Elmer Boyd reopened the speedway in 1982, featuring late model, hobby, and sportsman classes at the track. A lot of the popular dirt late model drivers at the time made stops at Boyd's Speedway (Tennessee-Georgia.) They included, Scott Bloomquist, Jeff Purvis, John Gill, "Little" Bill Corum, Jerry Inmon, Red Farmer and Larry Moore. The track's other classes were dominated by local drivers, Milton Brown, Jack Harper, and Kenny LeCroy. In addition to the regular racing programs, the Southern All-Stars made a number of appearances during the mid-80's. The 1984 Southern All-Stars Point Champion, Jerry Inmon of Mississippi, won two races and Edwin Anthony had a win in the dirt series. Later, Elmer Boyd would form a partnership with Winchester Speedway to host Special weekend racing events. Winchester would race on Saturday nights, while Boyd's would race on Sunday nights or Sunday afternoons. This worked out really well for both tracks; bringing in a good field of late models for each track, according to Elmer Boyd. The speedway was again closed at the end of the 1992 season.

Tennessee-Georgia Speedway (Boyd's) would reopen in 1993 under the ownership of Ken Gravitt and Herschel McKee. At the time, the track ran a weekly program that featured limited late models and several other classes. In 1995 McKee became the sole operator/promoter of the speedway and ran a weekly racing program, usually consisting of limited late models and four of five other classes of race cars. I attended a lot of races at the track in the mid-90's and saw some of the best limited late model races in the area at the time. I remember some really good races involving Rick Hixson, Kenny LeCroy, Brian Burke, and a number of other limited late model drivers. McKee ran the track until the early 2000's, according to Elmer Boyd. However, the grand old track was in bad need of some remodeling and some updates to both, the track and the spectator areas.

Since that first race in October of 1952 the track has undergone a number of name changes over the years, Chattanooga Raceway Park, Chattanooga International Speedway, Stateline Speedway, and Tennessee-Georgia Raceway. However, to most race fans who have been to the track it will always be, Boyd's Speedway.

In 2007, George Shaw and Russ Ruskin, became the new owners of Boyd's. Perhaps, the single best thing the new owners did, in their short ownership of the track, was bring back the super late models to the race fans of Boyd's Speedway. A new super late model track record was set during this time, a lap of 13.91. However, the track was closed that same year.

In 2008 the best thing that ever happened to the grand old speedway did. The Harvey Brothers, Robert and Richard, came to the rescue of Boyd's Speedway. Long time fans of dirt track racing, the two brothers, in my opinion and the opinion of many others, saved the famed speedway on Scruggs Road. They completely upgraded the race track, adding concrete walls, new clay to the surface, painted and repaired other areas of the track. In the spectator areas they completely remodeled the bathrooms, converted the concession area to restaurant style equipment, remodeled the scoring tower, and replaced and added new bleachers. In short the track had a rebirth thanks to the Harvey Brothers. On my first trip to the track after all the work had been completed, I person-

Looking toward turn one at Boyd's Speedway in 2015. (Photo provided by the author)

ally thanked them for making Boyd's, once again, a top notch dirt racing facility. During their ownership several regional dirt touring series brought great super late model racing to the track, they included Southern Regional Racing Series, and the Southern All-Stars Racing Series. They also had one of the best weekly racing programs in the region. This crowd pleasing program included, steel head late models, crate late models, street, and hobby classes.

In 2014, National Boiler Service owner, David Duplissey, and long time super late model dirt track ace, Dale McDowell bought the track from the Harvey Brothers. They continue make improvements to the facility, adding more seating and continue to improve the pit areas. The new owners have changed the race night from Friday to Saturday nights to make it more convenient for the race fans and drivers. The annual "Cabin Fever" race is still held in early February. Also, they still have a number of regional dirt touring series events at the track, including the Southern All-Stars, Ray Cook's Spring Nationals; and in 2015, the Old Man's Garage Spring Nationals. In addition, Dale McDowell operates a driving school at the track. Dale, David, and General Manager Mark Wooten's future goals are to provide an excellent racing program for the drivers and race fans, and hopefully have a national touring series event like the Lucas Oil or the World of Outlaws in the not too distant future.

Boyd's Speedway will always have a special place in my heart. Every time I set in the stands or visit the drivers in the pits, I think back to "Wild Man" Jerry Smith winning that first race I attended some sixty years ago; the famous Boyd's chicken sandwiches my dad and I ate at the track, and the many famous drivers I have seen race at this speedway over the last 60 years, ahhh the memories.

DIXIE SPEEDWAY

In 1969, legendary race driver Bud Lunsford and Cherokee County businessman Max Simpson opened a 3/8 mile red clay oval known as Dixie Speedway. The Speedway is located off highway 92 in Woodstock, Georgia. In its inaugural season it witnessed large

A view of the huge scoring tower and press box at Dixie Speedway. (Photo provided by Nick Nicholson)

crowds of race fans and perhaps the best field of late model drivers ever assembled at a single speedway. Drivers like, Doug Kenimer, Leon Sells, Charlie Mincey, and Buck Simmons raced so close that a split second slip going into a turn could cause the leader to go from first to fifth in a blink of an eye. Buck Simmons dominated the track that first year, winning an amazing 18 of 22 features, in the Speedy Evans # 41 black and gold Chevelle.

In 1972 Lunsford sold his interest in the track to Simpson. A short time later, Max had the track paved because of the success Jeffco Speedway, about 60 miles away, was having and hoped to follow suit. During the asphalt era some memorable moments were witnessed at the track. Those included; Bill Elliot's first win as a driver, beating legendary asphalt ace, Ronnie Sanders. Also, NASCAR stars like, Richard Petty, Bobby Allison, and David Pearson came to do battle with Jody Ridley. Ridley dominated the track while it was paved, winning 46 races. Finally, the famous match race between Bill Elliott and Dale Earnhardt, won by Earnhardt before the largest crowd ever to witness an event at the Speedway.

As the oil crisis of the mid-70's came, attendance started to take a downturn and the track was in need of major repairs. Rome Speedway owner, Mickey Swims, bought the track in 1976. Swims tried a number of promotional ideas to revive the track to no avail. Mickey saw the success of his Rome Speedway and decided to take up the asphalt and make Dixie a dirt facility once again. This proved to be one of the best decision Mickey ever made. His race car counts increase dramatically, along with a dramatic increase in race fans.

In 1978, two important developments occurred that greatly impacted the future of both of Mickey Swims' race tracks. First, he purchased yet another track, West Atlanta Raceway, and formed what came to be known as, the "Tri-Racing Circuit." In this circuit Swims ran West Atlanta on Friday Nights, Dixie on Saturday nights, and Rome on Sunday. Later, he decided to sell West Atlanta in the late '80's, and keep the Dixie and Rome speedways. Secondly, and perhaps most importantly to the future of the two remaining tracks; Mickey decided become a stop on Robert Smawley's new National Dirt Racing Association (NDRA) in 1978, with $10,000 payouts for 100 lap late model events. A total of eight NDRA races were held at the track; with Jeff Purvis, Larry Moore, and Stan Massey winning two each, while Buck Simmons and Bud Lunsford had one win each.

Throughout the '80's Dixie Speedway was one of the premier racing facilities in the South. Hosting one of the best weekly racing programs in the country, with as many as five to seven classes, including one of the best dirt late model programs in the South. Throughout the 80's, regional racing series like, B.J. Parker's Southern All-Stars Racing Series were yearly events at the track.

In 1990, Mickey, his son Mike, and the legendary race announcer Jimmy Mosteller started the Hav-A-Tampa racing series; the brain child of all three; with Dixie Speedway as its home track. That year the first two races held at Dixie were won by Bill Ingram and Tony Reaid. During its time, the series visited many tracks throughout the South including; the Cherokee Speedway in Gaffney, S.C; to the Smoky Mountain Speedway in Maryville, TN;

to the South Hampton (VA.) Speedway; to the Columbus (Miss.) Speedway; to Jax Raceway in Jacksonville, Fla., and many others. However, the final race was always held at Dixie Speedway. That final race was the high paying, Hav-A-Tampa Shootout which attracted the best dirt late model drivers in the country. Mickey said that the 1995 Shootout was perhaps the best late model dirt race he has ever seen. Most of the top late model drivers were in the field. The race was won by Batesville Arkansas's, Bill Fry. The track had two grooves, the high groove was rough; but super fast and Fry came all the way through the field on the rough top groove. On the final lap, Fry Never lifted and beat Scott Bloomquist, running the smooth low groove, at the finish line by about three feet.

Jimmy Mosteller stepped down from the series in 1999. Hav-A-Tampa's last year sponsoring the series was 2000. The series then became, UDTRA Pro DirtCar Series and continued, with Mike Swims as president, until the end of 2002. The series was then sold to Doug Bland and became the Xtreme DirtCar Series .

Today, the track continues to have very good crowds and top notch racing in all its divisions. The Lucus Oil Late Model Dirt Series makes regular visits to the speedway; along with regional dirt series like the Old Man's Garage Spring National Series under the direction of dirt late model ace, Ray Cook. Some of the records at the Dixie include, the late model track record of 13.80, currently held by Riley Hickman. Other records through 2014 include, Stan Massey with the most Late model wins, at 69; Jody Ridley, second with 56 wins (46 of those asphalt wins); Leon Sells, third with 47 wins; and Buck Simmons, fourth with 46 wins. Finally, a new red clay surface awaited both the drivers and race fans for the 2015 season.

This track has always been known for its famed Late model division and the many dirt late model legends who have taken the checkered flag at the historic speedway. On opening night 46 years ago the track began its journey into history; when the legendary Buck Simmons won the first late model race at Dixie Speedway. Thanks to the hard work and dedication of the Swims family I see this continuing long into the future.

ROME SPEEDWAY

Coming from the main entrance gate at Rome Speedway. (Photo provided by the author)

William Garner Snowden built the ½ mile red clay Rome Speedway in 1965 and '66. He opened the track because he was tired of traveling to race, and wanted a track closer to home. The track bills itself as the "World's Fastest Half-Mile Clay Track." Speeds at the ultra fast speedway reach over 120 miles per hour at times.

Legendary NASCAR driver Joe Lee Johnson of Chattanooga, Tennessee won the first late model race on September 4, 1966, out dueling Harold Fryar. The speedway ran three classes of race cars that opening day, late models, the super fast skeeters (won by Bud Lunsford), and the popular jalopy class (won by Fletcher Cavender). The track hosted a total of 5 races its opening season.

I made my first trip to, what was then Rome International Speedway, during the 1967 season, Bud Lunsford won the popular skeeter race that day, taking the checkered flag in one of his 97 victories at the Speedway. Lunsford is by far and away the all time wins leader at Rome, dominating the late models and skeeters during his illustrious career. The track boasts a historic list of drivers who have raced the famed ½ mile. They include, Buck

Simmons, Leon Sells, Charles Hughes, Jody Ridley, Leon Archer, Stan Massey, Charlie Mincey, and home town driver Henley Gray to name a few.

I made the trip to Rome many times with Jody Ridley over the years, while helping him in the pits. The texture of the red clay used at Rome was always a mystery to me. I found out years later from racing legend Charlie Mincey, that it was called, red brick clay and it was found in the areas around the Rome Speedway. Mincey said, "Rome's clay was the best I ever raced on during my career. It was so tacky that when you walked across it after a race to go get your money at the scoring tower, it would pull your shoes off if you were not careful." Dixie Speedway owner Mickey Swims, who bought the Rome Speedway in late 1968, uses this clay, not only on the track at Rome, but also trucks it to Dixie when its time to resurface that Speedway.

At one time, Rome was part of the Tri-Racing Circuit that included, West Atlanta Raceway, Dixie Speedway, and the Rome Speedway. During this time, Mickey Swims owned all three tracks. Swims later sold West Atlanta and now concentrates on running weekly races on Saturdays at Dixie, and special racing events at Rome on Sunday nights. Mickey has tried racing on a weekly basis at Rome, but has had mixed results. The track over the last several years has been running five to six racing shows a year. These events feature national and regional touring series super late model races. They include the national touring Lucas Oil Late Model Dirt Series; along with a number of regional tours like the Southern All-Stars Racing Series, the Schaeffer Oil Summer Nationals, And Ray Cook's Old Man's Garage Spring Nationals. This, along with having several local classes race during the events, has proven to be a winning formula for Swims.

In years past, Rome was a regular stop on the Hav-A-Tampa Dirt Racing Series. The tour, started by legendary announcer Jimmy Mosteller, Mickey, and his late son Mike Swims, made regular stops at the speedway. These races often set the stage for the big Hav-A-Tampa Shootout, the final race of the season always held at Dixie Speedway. Some of the big winners in the series at Rome were, Ronnie Johnson and Dale McDowell with three wins each, and Scott Bloomquist with two checkered flags, Phil Coltrane, Stan Massey, Ray Cook, Wendell Wallace, Earl Pearson Jr., Granger Howell, and Dan Schlieper also had wins. Finally, Robert Smawley's NDRA made a stop at Rome on April 20, 1980; and you guessed it, Bud Lunsford won the race in a thrilling last lap finish over Rodney Combs.

Today, Rome Speedway continues to hold exciting special event races throughout the year. The race fans and drivers still come; if for no other reason, the sheer high speeds of the race cars at the, "World's Fastest Half-Mile Clay Track."

TOCCOA (RACEWAY) SPEEDWAY

Sign at the entrance to Toccoa Speedway Billed as "the Fastest 1,650 Feet in Georgia." (Photo provided by the author)

It was during the early 70's that I visited Toccoa Speedway quite often. At the time, I was part of Jody Ridley's pit crew and we raced in the Northeast Georgia area quite often. Not only did we race the high banks of Toccoa Speedway, we also raced at nearby Hartwell and Lavonia as well. What I liked about the Toccoa Speedway was you seemed to go back into the 50's era of racing. It was like you were in the middle of the movie set filming, GREASED LIGHTNING. A movie about Windell Scott, especially the part about his early career in dirt track racing. The track is located in an area surrounded by several heavily wooded valleys in Stephens County, Georgia. At the time, the whole facility was simple in nature; from the simple spectator seating; to the most basic concession stand and restroom facilities. The red clay dirt track was "old school" in every aspect. Even today, it features J.R. Headen, a race driver in his mid-70's who has raced his #1X race car at the track for over forty years. Over the years, Headen has won a lot of races and several track championships at the speedway. He is always a crowd favorite among the young and old, and is still very competitive.

Toccoa Speedway was built in the early 1950's by Rufus Tribble. Garland Sheriff was the original owner and operator of the track. Willard Stamey took the very first checkered flag at Toccoa on May 7, 1955. That first season the track ran races until October of that year. Toccoa Speedway is the third oldest speedway in Georgia, only Savannah's Oglethorpe Speedway (1951) and Boyds Speedway (1952) in Ringgold, Georgia are older. However, Toccoa holds the distinction of being the longest continuously running dirt track in the state. "The Fastest 1,650 Feet of Dirt in Georgia," as the track bills itself, is celebrating its 60th year in 2015.

According to long time track announcer, Charles Head, Garland Sheriff built the track for two reasons. The first, was for his brother Cleo, an aspiring race car driver, to have a place to practice. Sheriff also wanted to have a race track with the idea of holding stock car races in the future. L.B. Berryman and Johnny Sheriff promoted races at the track in the '60's and into the '70's still under the ownership of Garland.

According to Charles, sometime in the early '80's, the Victor Christian family purchased the track. Around 1982, James Browner began promoting races at Toccoa. He ran the speedway until the late '80's. Toward the end of the '80's, Franklin North Carolina's Randy McCoy secured a lease on the track. McCoy promoted the track for a few years until the mid-90's, running several classes of race cars.

The mid-90's also saw Carnesville Georgia's David Pritchett gain a lease on the Speedway from the Christian family. He promoted the speedway for about three years. Around 1997, Toccoa's Dean Hill was the last promoter to actively run the speedway with any success during the '90's. However, in 1999 Ricky Holbrook from Toccoa did have the track for a six month period, closing the track in the middle of '99.

The 2000's saw the Christian family lease the track to South Carolina's James Gibson. In 2002 it was David Pritchett's turn to reopen the speedway, running the high banked speedway until around 2010. Randy McCoy and Leon Latham promoted the track in 2011 and 2012, hosting races in several classes. They also brought the FASTRAK Racing Series to the speedway. In 2013, Asheville, North Carolina's Andy McCoy obtained a lease from the Christian family estate. McCoy and track manager Brad York had big plans for the speedway. However, those plans never materialized for some reason. Over the years, most of the promoters had ignored the old track's need of some "tender loving care." Through the years, things like, renovations, painting, and upgrades were almost totally ignored. The track had almost reached the point where it might not survive.

It would have been a shame for this old high banked speedway to have become only a memory. Toccoa Speedway has a long and rich history in Southern dirt racing. Over her 60 years, drivers like, Willard Stamey, Wayne Coffee, Tommy Irwin, George Roberts, Charlie Mincey, Tootle Estes, Steve "Hot Rod" Lamance, Ronnie Johnson, Buck Simmons, Jody Ridley, Bud Lunsford, Doug Kenimer, Leon Sells, C.L. Pritchett, Ray Cook, David Payne, Casey Roberts, Jonathan Davenport, and many others, have challenged the red clay high banks of Toccoa. The track has also been the site of many Southern All-Star Races, with Dennis Franklin, Ray Cook, Chris Madden, Randy Weaver, Jonathan Davenport, Casey Roberts, and Randy Hemphill, some of the drivers scoring wins in the series. Several years ago, up and coming late model driver, Duayne Hommel recorded one of his last checkered flags at Toccoa before an automobile accident ended his career. In 1993 and '94, legendary race announcer; and everybody's, "Little, Biddy,

Buddy," Jimmy Mosteller, brought the Hav-A-Tampa Dirt Racing Series to Toccoa Speedway. The big winners in those races were Tim Headen and Ronnie Johnson. Finally, the current track record for late models drivers is held by Chris Ferguson at 11.764.

However, as the old saying goes, "Help is on the way." In 2014, Lula Georgia's Husband and wife team, Mike and Jackie Davidson, signed a long term lease on Toccoa Speedway. The Davidson's have turned, what was a track in bad need of updates and repairs, into a modern dirt racing facility. Through a lot of hard work, Mike and Jackie have built new concession and restroom acilities; installed modern fencing throughout the speedway; added safety guard railing around the track; modernized the scale house and pit areas, along with many other improvements. In 2015, Mike Davidson announced the speedway will be sanctioned under the FASTRAK Racing Series for the year. The track Plans to hold a number of FASTRAK races, along with Ultimate Super Late Model events.

A look across the track from the main outside pits at Toccoa. (Photo provided by the author)

I made my first trip to Toccoa Speedway in over forty years for the FASTRAK racing series event last Saturday (6-6-15) night. I liked what has happened to the grand old high banked speedway. It has been transformed into a modern dirt racing facility. It is now perhaps one of the best racing venues in the South. However, it still retains that warm welcome feel you get from every one at the track. The fans are real Southern race fans; and the Toccoa staff still sees to it that you have a good old time at the race track.

CHEROKEE SPEEDWAY

The Legendary Cherokee Speedway in Gaffney, S.C, looking toward the main grandstands from the back straight-away. (Photo provided by Deborah Perry)

Cherokee Speedway, one of the South's most historic dirt tracks, was built by J. A. Mobley in 1957. Mobley was the owner of I-85 Truck Stop at the time and wanted to try his hand promoting a race track. However, Mobley soon realized that the racing business was not for him. It was then, that Edgar "Hard Rock" Gault worked out a year by year verbal agreement with Mobley to operate the race track. After Mobley's death in July of 1981; Gault was unable to reach an agreement with the Mobley estate during the Winter and the track sat idle for the first time in its history.

Then in mid-82, local Gaffney tire dealer and former race driver David Perry and his wife Deborah, were granted a short-term lease on the track. They renovated the speedway, remodeling the concession and restroom facilities, and painted throughout the speedway. The Perry's had good car counts and fan support during the remainder of that season. The new promoters wanted a racing class where local drivers could afford to field a race car on a small budget. Deborah recently told me, "We were trying to come up with a name for this new division, and all at once a thunderstorm came up, with a lot of thunder and lightning. So right then we decided to call it the Thunder and Lightning Class." The division was a huge success, with large car counts every race night. Deborah said, "That season for us was a great season and we had a lot of fun."

Cherokee Speedway as it looked as a ½ mile track, note the down hill back straight-away, where speeds were sometimes approaching 130 mph. (Photo provided by Deborah Perry)

After the legal issues were settled with the Mobley estate, Gault was able to obtain the property and resumed his owner/promoter duties at the speedway. The Perry's again came forward and were able to obtain another lease on the track for the 1986 season. During the Perry's promotion of the track, the old speedway enjoyed some of her best years. The Perry's had several weekly racing divisions including, late models, limited late models, and several other classes. A new "Bomber" division was also introduced. It turned out to be the track's largest division, with car counts of over 60 cars at times. David Perry, being a former driver, was able to understand the racing business from both sides of the fence. Deborah worked the gate and concessions at the speedway, always listening to the race fans and their ideas.

It was during the Perry's ownership of the track, that I taught at USC-Union and was at the Cherokee Speedway about every Saturday night. I remember one of the things I enjoyed, that Deborah started at the speedway, was during special event races she would play upbeat music on the public address system before the feature races. I remember one song in particular, it was "Tonight, Tonight" by Phil Collins. Man that song always got me and the whole crowd ready for a big late model race. Also, Danny Goins, the track announcer would come down track side and introduce the late model drivers to the crowd before a special event feature race. Finally, it was during a limited late model race in '88 that me and two of my racing buddies were sitting in lawn chairs on the top row of the stands; and on the last lap coming out of turn four, Ricky Weeks, Wally Fowler, and Petey Ivy all side touched one another. The result was something I'll probably never see again, a backward one-two-three finish. Don't ask me the order of finish.

In January of 1989, two North Carolina businessmen, Ernie Elkins and Terry Brotherton, obtained the lease from the Perry's. The two men published a racing magazine (Racing News) in Charlotte, NC, and were familiar with the track. Both men were excited about promoting the track and continued to operate it until Brotherton sold his part around 1999. Elkins became the sole owner of the speedway until he sold the track to Lenny Buff and his son, Seth in 2003. It was also in '03 that the Buff's shortened the track from a ½ mile to again its original size if 3/8 of a mile. This has had mixed reviews among both, drivers and race fans. The track once billed as, "The South's Fastest 1/2-Mile Dirt Track" was just that, until the track was shortened. The wide turns; along with its high banks; and the down hill backstretch made it possible for super late model drivers to reach speeds of over 130 mph.

During her almost 58 years, Cherokee Speedway has seen its share of famous late model drivers like, Mike Duvall, Freddie Smith, Scott Bloomquist, Buck Simmons, Ed Gibbons, Steve "Hot Rod" Lamance, Jack Pennington, and Jeff Purvis to name but a few. Even future NASCAR stars such as, Dale Earnhardt, Bill Elliott, and the Allison brothers, Bobby and Donnie, have toured the red clay of this historic track.

A new crop of super late model drivers are ready to join them in the history of Cherokee Speedway. Those dirt warriors include, Chris Madden, Jonathan Davenport, Dennis Franklin, Casey Roberts, Chris Ferguson, and others. These new drivers and the hundreds of loyal fans who turn out each week at the track will carry on Cherokee's rich history. Finally, the track continues to hold its annual events like, March Madness, the Stick Elliott Memorial, and the Blue/Gray 100. The regional tours still make several trips to Cherokee; the Southern All-Stars Racing Series; and the Carolina Clash Super Late Model series among them. Also, the Lucas Oil Late Model Dirt Series continues make the speedway one of its annual stops. The future looks bright for the 58 year old red clay oval. Cherokee Speedway is still today one of the best dirt tracks in the South.

Red Clay & Dust

CHAPTER FIVE:
THE DIRT WARRIORS OF THE PAST

This chapter takes a close look at some of the legendary "dirt warriors" of the past. Most of these drivers are either in the National Dirt Late Model Hall of Fame or in their States' Racing Hall of Fame. These are but a few of the famed dirt late model drivers that have raced the dirt tracks of the South. Each of these drivers is worthy of an entire book devoted to their lives and their contribution to Southern dirt racing.

BUCK SIMMONS

A young Buck Simmons driving for Day Chevrolet. (Photo provided by Leon Sells)

Charles Leroy "Buck" Simmons was born on July 31, 1946 in Baldwin, Ga. Buck began hanging around the Banks County

Speedway at the age of 12. At age 14 Simmons started driving the speedway's water truck. Later, he got his own car and drove on the track before the weekly races on Saturdays. Buck's first career win came at a small track in Westminster, S.C.

I saw Buck for the first time at Dixie Speedway in Woodstock, Georgia in the early 70's. I had been around dirt racing for quite a while and knew right away that the driver of the Speedy Evans owned black and gold #41 Chevelle was perhaps the best late model dirt driver I had ever seen.

Around this time most drivers wore no racing suits, usually just a comfortable pair of pants and a T-shirt. Simmons always wore black pants and a black T-shirt, and that famous white racing helmet with the classic "bubble shield." In order to keep the dust out of a driver's mouth and nose, most drivers used a long scarf to wrap around their mouth and noise. Buck had a long bright red scarf that he used. It was one Saturday night at Dixie that I was standing with Jody Ridley's brother, Biddle, behind the pit wall watching the distances between race cars. Buck was leading the race in his black and gold #41, going into turns one and two leading by several car lengths. The car was in a power slide and about two feet of Buck's red scarf was blowing out the window. I looked over at Biddle and said, "Look, it's the Red Baron."

Buck Simmons was almost unbeatable in the early years of the famed Dixie Speedway. In 1969, the first year the speedway was open, Simmons won an amazing 18 out of the 22 features that year. He did this racing against some of the toughest competition of the period. Saturday night after Saturday night he out dueled the likes of Leon Sells, Doug Kenimer, and others in his Da-Je Mobile homes, Quality Motor Sales #41.

Tazewell Speedway owner Gary Hall once told me that when Buck was driving for Georgia car owner Brad Hendricks, the car owner tried to get "show money" (money track owners paid to get certain drivers just to show up) from Atomic Speedway owner Bob Martin for Buck just to show up at Atomic. Bob told him he did not pay "show money" he only collected money and filled stands with race fans. Hendricks finally gave in and brought Buck to Atomic, arriving late but Martin did allow Buck to qualify. He won the pole and went on to win the feature that night, but received no "show money" from Bob Martin.

Buck teamed up with several legendary car owners during his long racing career. After driving the Speedy Evans race car, Simmons drove for Cherokee County businessman Max Simpson, one of the early owners and founders of Dixie Speedway. Buck also drove some of the first late models built by Barry Wright Race cars, located in Cowpens, South Carolina.

Simmons also raced on the asphalt tracks around the South, especially after Dixie Speedway was paved. His asphalt ability was good enough to earn rides on the NASCAR Winston Cup Circuit (now Sprint Cup). Buck made eight NASCAR Winston Cup career starts. Hiss best finish was a 14th at Atlanta Motor Speedway in 1979, driving a Kennie Childers-owned car.

However, Simmons first love was dirt racing, and it was on the dirt short tracks where his true talent shined. Buck beat some of the best dirt drivers the sport had to offer. Jody Ridley, H.E. Vineyard, Charles Hughes, Tootle Estes, Bud Lunsford, and Charlie Mincey were among the many drivers Simmons out dueled on dirt tracks all over the nation.

Larry Moore, a teammate of Simmons when both drove for Jim Erp (Tri-City Aluminum) during the NDRA era once said, "Most drivers set up the car to their driving style. Buck adapts his driving skills to the car no matter the setup."

Among Buck's many accomplishments were; his wins at Montgomery Motor Speedway's Alabama 200; the Rattler 100 at South Alabama Speedway; the 1981 NDRA Championship; and the 1985 NDRA $250,000 Invitational winner, taking home a $30,000 payday. Simmons was the NDRA's all time wins leader with 23 victories. Buck also scored wins in the Hav-A-Tampa, and the Southern All Stars Series. Simmons was the first inductee into the National Dirt Late Model Hall of Fame in 2001. He was later inducted into the Georgia Racing Hall of Fame in 2009.

Buck Simmons, "the living legend," scored win number 1000 at Lavonia Speedway in May of 2002, driving for his last car owner, Carnesville Georgia's Gerald Voyles in the John Deere green #41. After five decades, Simmons climbed out of the legendary #41 for the last time in 2003, having 1,012 wins to his credit, the last 31 of those in the Voyles race car.

Sadly, Buck Simmons passed away on August 12, 2012. Buck Simmons was a "living legend' in Southern dirt racing history. He was perhaps the best of the best.

HERBERT "TOOTLE" ESTES

Tootle Estes with one of his many checkered flags. (Photo courtesy of Paul's Auto Parts)

Herbert Estes was born during the "Great Depression" era on February 2, 1930. It was his grandmother, Beatrice, who gave Estes the nickname, "Tootle," a character in *The Little Golden Book Series For Kids* from the 1940's. Tootle was a little train engine involved in several adventures during the book series. Somehow Beatrice must have foreseen her grandson's future. In the book one of the lines read, "Green flag means go," and go Tootle Estes did. Beginning in the 1950's, until his death in 1982, Estes won races in about every kind of race car with four wheels. Estes drove Jalopies, Skeeters, NASCAR Sportsman, NASCAR Cup Series, and late models to over 1200 wins, according to the late Herman Collins the West Haven Auto Parts founder and former car owner of Estes.

Tootle had between 200 and 300 of his wins in the dirt late models, racing at dirt tracks all over the South. Some of those tracks included, Atomic Speedway, Volunteer Speedway (Bull's Gap), Boyd's Speedway, Gadsden Speedway, 411 Speedway, and Smokey Mountain Speedway. It was at Maryville's Smokey Mountain Speedway where I first saw Tootle Estes race. It was Saturday night May 27, 1967. I was just 17 years old and had been an avid race fan for a while. My wife and I had just eloped and gotten married and I convinced her that what better place to spend our honeymoon than watching a dirt late model race. Estes won the feature race with ease that night besting a strong field of cars that included L.D. Ottinger, Jim Hunter, and others. He was driving a bright yellow and red #28 Ford Fairlane with a big red woodpecker on its side, and a 427c.i. engine under the hood. Later, I found out the race car belonged to Woody Bradley a long time car and engine builder in the Knoxville area, who ran Woody's Auto Clinic at the time. So that explained why the woodpecker was on the car's side. To this day when I am attending a race at Smokey Mountain I have a little fun with the race fans by telling them I know quite a bit about the track history. I can tell them who won the race on May 27, 1967.

Tootle ran 12 NASCAR Grand National (now known as Sprint Cup) events and 4 NASCAR Convertible Series events. Estes had 4 top 10 finishes in the cup events and had 3 top 10 finishes in the convertibles. His first Grand National start was at Ashville-Weaverville, N.C. Tootle's best finish in Grand National was a 10th place finish in the famed Southern 500 at Darlington, S.C.

During Estes' racing career it was not uncommon for drivers to race four or five times a week. So drivers were able to rack up large numbers of wins in a season. In his best year Estes won an unheard of 85 features out of 104 starts. Tootle raced quite a bit in

Georgia during the 1960's, driving the winged "skeeters" for Athens, Ga. native James "Jabo" Bradbury. However, it was in Georgia, while Estes was driving "Ace" Lawson's 32 Ford Sedan against the likes of Buck Simmons, Charlie Padgett, Leon Sells, T.C. Hunt, Harold Fryar, Bud Lunsford, and others that he was barred from racing in Georgia. Tootle won 16 straight events until he wrecked the car. After repairing the car, Tootle started another winning streak. During this streak Estes won races at tracks like the Peach Bowl in Atlanta, Toccoa Speedway, Banks County Speedway, and other Georgia tracks. The good old Georgia boys had just seen enough of the dirt warrior from Knoxville, Tennessee.

All through the 70's Estes raced in late models throughout the South. He drove late models for Paul's Auto Parts owner Tommy Hickman of Soddy Daisy, Tennessee during much of the 70's. During his time with Tommy Hickman they won a number of late model races at tracks all over Tennessee, Alabama, and Georgia. They won feature races at Atomic Speedway, Gadsden Speedway, Tazewell Speedway, 411 Speedway to name but a few.

Tommy's wife, Elizabeth, and I were talking one day and she told me a funny story. She said, when Tootle was racing for Paul's Auto Parts, on his trips to Soddy Daisy to visit and help with the race car, he always insisted on going to his favorite restaurant, The Hungry Fisherman, that was located in East Ride, Tennessee. Estes loved the peel and eat shrimp that was always on the menu. Elizabeth said, "Tootle would eat so many of the shrimp that the peeled skins were piled so high on his plate that other customers were staring at Estes and the people at his table." She said she got embarrassed at the strange looks they received on numerous occasions.

After driving the Paul's Auto Parts sponsored car through much of the 70's, Tootle drove late models for a number of other car owners. Those owners included, Herman Collins, Bill Ogle Sr. and the last was Butch Curtis. It was in the Curtis late model that Tootle Estes would win his last race. The race was at Volunteer Speedway on the night of August 20, 1982. Estes had won the race and after some side by side racing with "Little" Bill Corum and others; he got out of the car complaining of severe arm pain. Tootle died later that night of a massive heart attack, he was just 52 years old.

During his long racing career he was one of the toughest to beat on dirt tracks throughout the South, no matter what kind of race car he was driving.

Tootle won several late model track championships during his career. Among them were, three late model titles at Atomic Speedway, two NASCAR Sportsman titles at Smokey Mountain Speedway, and one title at the last track he would drive on, the Volunteer Speedway. A few of Estes major dirt late model wins include; the 1974 Firecracker 75 at Gadsden, Alabama; the 1975 Hall of Fame 100 at Atomic Speedway near Knoxville, Tennessee; and the 1980 Volunteer 100 at the Volunteer Speedway at Bull's Gap, Tennessee. In 2009 Tootle Estes was inducted into both the National Dirt Late Model Hall of Fame and the Georgia Racing Hall of Fame. Tootle Estes was truly "the little engine that could."

JACK BOGGS

I saw Jack Boggs race for the first time at Atomic Speedway in 1983, at the Hall of Fame 100. Boggs went on to win this big money race, as he did so many others during his career. When a

"Black" Jack Boggs' Late model ready for the 100 lap race at Atomic Speedway. (Photo by Nick Nicholson)

lot of money was on the line "Black" Jack Boggs was a sure bet to be in the thick of the battle for the win. Muriel Jackson Boggs was born was born in Webbville, Kentucky on April 4, 1950. He would go on to become one of the best dirt late model drivers to ever strap into a race car.

In 1978 Boggs watched a race at Southern Ohio Raceway and knew he wanted to become a race car driver. After a brief stint as a hobby driver, Jack started competing in late models at Ashland Kentucky's, Checkered Flag Speedway, and at the Southern Ohio Raceway.

In 1980 two important events would help launch Jack's career into the national spotlight. First, Black Shamrock Coal Company's Garland Flaugher, offered to sponsor Boggs. Then he was introduced to the famed race car builder, Whiteland Indiana's, C.J. Rayburn. In 1981, at the Southeastern Winner Nationals, Jack won in his first race with his Flaugher/Rayburn sponsored late model. During the '81 Speed Weeks in Florida, Boggs did what few drivers have been able to do. He went the entire week without having to compete in a heat race. Jack was able to qualify in the top three each night. Thus, assuring himself a spot in the feature without competing in a single heat race. In 1982 Jack would race in Smawley's National Dirt Racing Association (NDRA). Boggs would go on to win three NDRA events including, the NDRA's "Super Bowl of Dirt Racing," in Pontiac, Michigan seen by over 30,000 race fans.

The one thing I remember about "Black" Jack was his fierce never give up attitude. A race I witnessed at Mount Vernon Kentucky's, Rockcastle Speedway in the mid-80's (when the track was dirt) best demonstrates this temperament. H.E. Vineyard was leading over John Gill, and would go on to win the race. However, Boggs was involved in a wreck and his car was clearly damaged; but Boggs was turning laps as fast as the leaders, although he was laps down and clearly out of contention for the win. It was this never give up attitude that was key to many of Jack's biggest wins which included, three Dirt Track World Championships in ('84', '90,' '95'); three Hillbilly 100's ('85,' '86,' '87'); the North-South 100; two Winchester (VA) 200's ('84,' and '96'); the Spring 100, at Concord, NC; the famed World 100 in 1995, and many others.

Boggs had some of his greatest dirt late model success in the STARS series. Jack won his first STARS race at Log Cabin (VA) Raceway in 1984, and his last STARS win came at the Florence (KY) Speedway at the Bluegrass Nationals in his familiar #B4 in 1997. In between these Stars wins he would go on to win 25 others, finishing third on their all time wins list with 27 feature wins.

In 1999 Boggs sold his racing operation and drove C.J. Rayburn's house car. In some of his last races, during Speedweeks 2000, Jack competed in STARS and UDTRA events, driving the Rayburn house car to a fifth place finish in a STARS event. During his career "Black" Jack Boggs will always be remembered for his never give up attitude, which made him a crowd favorite among race fans all over the country.

Jack Boggs won around 450 races during his legendary racing career. His racing achievements and the high profile big money wins will be very hard to duplicate by any driver in the near future. Unfortunately, on March 27, 2000, "Black" Jack Boggs was killed just nine days short of his 50th birthday. He will be missed by his family. But most of all the sport of dirt racing lost one of the best dirt late model drivers to ever come out of the bluegrass state of Kentucky. Jack Boggs was as the old saying goes, a "What you see is what you get" type of guy. Boggs was posthumously inducted into the inaugural class of the National Dirt Late Model Hall of Fame in 2001.

CHARLIE MINCEY

A lot has been written about Charlie Mincey's well known moonshining exploits over the years. This begs the question, did Charlie learn his driving skills from hauling whiskey; or was he just born with the ability to drive a race car? Either way Charlie Mincey would become one of the best dirt track drivers in the South. Mincey's career spanned four decades, beginning in 1950, and lasting until his last race in 1982.

Charlie Mincey was born in the "rough" Bellwood section of Atlanta, Georgia on November 19, 1931. After hauling moonshine as a teenager for several years, his dad and others were becom-

Charlie Mincey in the Levi Day Chevrolet at Rome Speedway in 1970. (Photo courtesy of Charlie Mincey)

ing fearful that his luck of never getting caught hauling whiskey might soon run out. So in 1950, in order to get Mincey away from the shine business, "Bad-Eye" Shirley decided to let Charlie drive a Billy Hester built jalopy car that he owned at the Peach Bowl in Atlanta. The Peach Bowl was a ¼ mile race track that had just recently opened. Mincey responded by winning the first two races he entered. The track officials bumped Charlie up to the sportsman division (this class had more experienced drivers and the race engines were larger) at the track. Mincey won his first race in that division also, besting the legendary Jack Smith.

In 1954, after dominating most of the racing events at the Peach Bowl for about four years, race track owner and promoter Roy Shoemaker had seen enough. He offered Mincey a ride in his 1934 Ford race car. Charlie proved Shoemaker had made the right decision by winning 22 out 25 feature races. Later, the car was sold to Cole Avery of Cummings, Georgia. He kept Mincey as the driver, but it was a short career with Avery. On his first race for Cole he blew the engine, while racing at the old half-mile Gainesville Speedway. Thus, ending his one race career with Avery.

In the early 60's, Charlie raced in what became known as a "Skeeter" (open-wheel modified with a wing on top) race car. Charlie raced "Skeeters" all over the South at tracks like Rome Speedway, Boyd's Speedway, and the Athens Speedway, against drivers like the legendary Bud Lunsford and others. After getting "burned out" from racing Charlie took a break in 1964.

Then in 1965 C.P. Shaw offered Mincey a ride in his new black 1932 Ford cut down sedan race car. When Charlie showed up at the Athens Speedway the car was race ready right down to Mincey's #16. Charlie could not turn the offer down. The Mincey-Shaw team went on to win a number of feature races at the Athens Speedway and the Peach Bowl.

In the late 60's, more and more drivers started turning to late model dirt racing. Mincey followed suit, starting with a 1955 Chevy and later to Chevelles, Novas, and finally Camaros. The first team Charlie raced for was the Leon Sells/Ed Massey team. It became a two car team, with both blue 1955 Chevy's carrying the #77 and sponsored by Quality Motor Sales. Mincey and Sells raced at different tracks each weekend during the racing season, trying to win as many races as possible. Later, Mincey drove for Jimmy Summerour at the Peach bowl and part-time for Webb Whitfield.

It was during the 1968 season that Buck Simmons and Charlie Mincey swapped race cars. Buck took Charlie's 1955 Chevy and Mincey took Buck's 1964 Chevelle, owned by Speedy Evans of Cummings, Georgia. Over a 10 race span Charlie won 8 races and Buck won the other 2 races. Evans offered Mincey the ride, but Charlie had already agreed to drive for the Day Chevrolet race team and Jack Diemer. Mincey drove the orange #16 Day Chevrolet for about seven years, winning races at Dixie Speedway, West Atlanta Raceway, and the Rome Speedway, to name a few.

Charlie recently told me a funny story. It was while Charlie and Leon Sells were both racing at the old Lakewood Speedway in

Atlanta in the 70's, that this occurred. Leon had left the race early due to mechanical problems and was asked by the track management to drive the pace car for the remainder of the race. It was only a short time before Mincey also was beset by mechanical problems and forced to leave the race. There had been a large number of caution flags and Sells was tired of driving the pace car. Sells asked Charlie to take over the pace car. Being the good sport he was, Mincey, along with two of his friends, jumped into the pace car and headed onto the track because of a wreck. As Charlie was coming down the long front straight-away he passed the only inlet to the pits, thinking there would be another lap of caution. As they were just entering turn one, the friend in the back seat said, "Charlie, I think the flagman just waved the green flag." Charlie looked back and sure enough here comes the field of race cars at full song. Charlie said, "I stomped the pedal to the floorboard of the new Mercury convertible pace car, trying to beat the field back to the pit inlet." Mincey said, "As we were in the middle of turns three and four, Freddy Fryar, who was leading the race, was waving his arm at us to move over and get out of the way. As the race cars were passing us on both sides, Jimmy Mosteller, the track announcer, was yelling over the track speakers to get those fools off the track." Mincey finally made it back to the pits after half the race field had blown by them. Charlie said his two passengers were, "white as ghosts."

In 1977 Mincey drove for Harold Hanson and Eddie Comber in a late model Camaro, built by Speedy Evans. Charlie raced what became known as, The Tri-Track Racing Circuit. Those tracks included, West Atlanta Raceway, Dixie Speedway, and Rome Speedway. Charlie was so dominate in the Evans car that they were asked to race somewhere else "for a while." They took their winning road show to Boyd's Speedway in Chattanooga, Tennessee and the Cleveland Speedway in Cleveland, Tennessee.

In 1980 Mincey drove for Soddy Daisy, Tennessee's, Tommy Hickman in the Paul's Auto Parts sponsored Camaro. This would be the last ride of his long and successful racing career. Charlie said, "This was perhaps one of the best cars I ever raced." After racing for a while, he called Tommy and told him he had just lost interest in driving a race car and asked Tommy to get another driver. Mincey had made up his mind to retire from racing.

However, on a Saturday in 1982, Luther Carter called Mincey and asked him to drive his race car at Dixie Speedway that night. Luther had severely burned his hand while taking the radiator cap off a hot race engine. Charlie had been out of racing since 1980, but agreed to help his old friend out and drive the car. Mincey qualified second fastest to Stan Massey, now driving Charlie's old ride, the Day Chevrolet. The race was a close one, with Stan Massey winning the feature and Charlie finishing a very close second. Mincey told me, "It was kind of ironic that the last race I would ever drive, I ended up getting beat by my old race car."

During Charlie's long and successful racing career he won over 600 races, sometimes 40 or 50 feature wins a year. Mincey won a number of track championships during his career at tracks that included, West Atlanta Raceway, the Peach Bowl, and Senoia Speedway. He also won the Georgia Modified State Championship in 1955; and the Georgia NASCAR Sportsman State Championship in 1959. In 2004 Charlie Mincey was inducted into the Georgia Racing Hall of Fame. If you see Mincey and his wife at Dixie Speedway or the Rome Speedway, don't fail to talk racing with him. "Old Charlie" has a lot of good racing stories he would be glad to share with you.

LEON ARCHER

Known in dirt racing circles as, "the man who made the triple digit number popular," Leon Archer was born in Griffin, Georgia on December 27, 1939. Archer came to the dirt late model scene in 1967, as the sport was exploding onto the scene in metro Atlanta and the surrounding areas. New dirt racing facilities were opening all over the area. They included, Rome speedway, a half mile clay oval, located in Rome, Georgia; Dixie Speedway a 3/8 mile clay track in Woodstock, Georgia; and finally, West Atlanta Raceway a red clay oval, located in Douglasville, Georgia. These new dirt tracks along with older tracks, like Turner Speedway (The Mountain); and Senoia Speedway, south of Atlanta made the area a

Leon Archer in the #222 taking another win. (Photo courtesy of Leon Archer)

paradise for area dirt late model drivers like Buck Simmons, Leon Sells, Charlie Mincey, Mike Head, Roscoe Smith, and others.

Leon Archer began his dirt late model racing career at the old Zebulon Speedway in 1967. Archer's first late model victory came at the Newnan Speedway in 1968, in his famous 1955 Chevrolet # 222. Archer took pride in his race cars, building most of the from the ground up, piece by piece. Leon recently told me, "I liked racing back during the 60's and 70's, heck you could take a cutting torch and a welder and a few tools and build a car. With a lot of hard work you could have a good handling race car." Archer went on to say, "I liked fooling with the chassis set-ups, that was the key to the whole race car." The best handling car I ever had was stolen at Atomic Speedway during my first year running the NDRA. I never had another car that I built that handled as good as that race car." Throughout his racing career Leon enjoyed working on his race cars, changing things and figuring out how to make his cars faster. He enjoyed that aspect of the sport as much as he liked driving the cars. Racing was a full-time business for him, working from Monday until race time on the weekends.

Archer always liked to run where the competition was the toughest. Leon said, "Competition was always strong at the little Cummings Speedway (Turner Speedway). A few of my fellow racers from Newnan went up with me, but most of them never went back again. It was a tough little track to run and you had to beat Buck Simmons, heck he had a bounty on him up there." During the 70's Archer was a regular feature race winner at area tracks like, Dixie Speedway, Rome Speedway, Senoia Raceway, West Atlanta Raceway and East Alabama Motor Speedway. Archer and the # 222 Chevy were becoming a dominant racing force in the region.

However, Leon Archer was about to become a national racing force thanks to Robert Smawley, and his National Dirt Racing Association. In 1978 Smawley started the NDRA, with its national racing schedule and $10,000 to win purses. It was a 1979 NDRA race at Myrtle Beach (S.C.) Speedway where Archer would score the first of his four NDRA wins. The others were Anderson (S.C.) Motor Speedway, Jackson Tennessee Fairgrounds Speedway. The last was in 1981, at Volunteer Speedway in Bulls Gap,Tennessee. Leon was also the first NDRA Champion in 1979.

Archer also competed in the World 100 at Eldora Speedway in Rossburg, Ohio. The closest he came to winning Earl Baltes' famous race was a second place finish in 1979. After leaving the NDRA in the 80's Archer raced closer to home. Leon drove for Bill Plemons and Charles Prater and was a dominate force in the mid-80's, winning more than 30 races in less than 40 starts, according to some who followed Archer's racing career during the period. Leon also raced cars for the famed Barry Wright Race Cars, located in Cowpens, South Carolina. Archer was driving a late model race car for Fayetteville Georgia's Ricky Williams when he ran his last race in the late 80's,

During his career Leon Archer was one of the few dirt drivers to race his entire career in the dirt late model divisions, winning over 250 feature races. Archer was inducted into the National Dirt Late Model Hall of Fame in 2003. Later, he was inducted into the Georgia Racing Hall of Fame in 2014. Most dirt race fans will always associate the iconic triple digit #222 with Leon Archer, the late model "dirt racing ace" from Griffin, Georgia.

MIKE DUVALL

Mike Duvall the "Flintstone Flyer" in action. (Photo by Nick Nicholson)

Cowpens, South Carolina's Mike Duvall, better known to dirt late model race fans as "The Flintstone Flyer," was perhaps one of the best dirt late model drivers the Palmetto State has ever produced. Duvall was born on July 6, 1949 in his hometown of Gaffney, South Carolina. When Mike was 15 years old and helping his uncle work on race cars, he took to the track one day in one of his uncle's cars. After a few hot laps around the track Duvall came in and parked the race car. Mike said after that driving experience, he only wanted to work around the shop and focus on playing football at Gaffney. At one time he had visions of playing in the NFL. However, a knee injury while playing football ended that short lived dream. This led Mike to make the decision to become a race car driver. It proved to be an unfortunate decision for Duvall's racing competition on the late model dirt tracks, and the rest, as the old saying goes, is history.

Mike's Racing career began in 1968, when he was half owner with Bobby Inman in his first race car. The car was a 1952 Ford, powered by a Danny Queen race engine. Duvall rose rapidly through a number of racing divisions before entering the dirt late model ranks. Mike started by racing in the "rookie" class, winning a total of 17 races in the two years he drove that division. In the "hobby" class he did even better, with 38 feature wins in just a year's time. Duvall climbed quickly through the sportsman ranks, finally moving up to the late model division.

Mike and his dad, Horace "Dick" Duvall, would develop a father-son racing team. They built a race shop and together built several race cars, with Mike's # 5 on them. A couple of the cars they built included, a solid gold 1963 Chevy Nova and a blue and yellow 1968 Chevy Camaro. The cars they built after that had his famous red and gold colors, and sported the racing # 5 on their sides. They raced as a team until Mike's father passed away.

In 1979 a man by the name of Dick Murphy would team with Duvall and change Mike's racing career forever. Together they would race in Robert Smawley's much talked about new National Dirt Racing Association (NDRA). This was the first national traveling series for dirt late models. It had large $10,000 pay outs to the winners of their 100 lap events, along with other bonus incentives. This was a deal too good to pass up and Murphy signed Mike to drive five NDRA races in 1979. After Duvall won three of the five races the two decided to team up for the 1980 racing season, and the "Flintstone Flyer" race car was introduced. The Flintstone cartoon character was on the car's hood when the 79 season ended. In 1980 Duvall was given the choice of keeping his # 5 or keeping his gold and red racing colors. Mike decided to keep his colors and the Flintstone Flyer race team was born, carrying the number F1. Interestingly, this was one of the first dirt late model race cars to have a letter in the car's number.

The car was always popular with the young race fans and the parents liked to snap photos of their children alongside the race car. In the late 80's while I was teaching at USC-Union, I watched

Mike race numerous times over the years at the Cherokee Speedway in Gaffney, S.C. There was one thing that I always admired in him. It made no difference to him if he won the race or had a bad night at the track, he always took time to talk to the race fans, especially the kids. I remember on several occasions he would stay at the track until every race fan had left the area of his car hauler. Over the years Duvall had a couple of beer companies offer him sponsorships but he turned them down. Mike said he felt he would not be doing the right thing for his young race fans.

For a number of years, Duvall has worked with the Shriners competing in a number of their races throughout the South. Mike has won several of these events and always gives half his winnings back to the Shriner's Hospitals for Children. Years ago a funny thing happened at one of these races. I was at a Shrine race at Laurens, S.C. in the late 80's. I happened to be at the race with "Big Larry" and "James," two of my racing buddies. Big Larry was sitting on one side of me next to a woman and her husband. It was about this time that Duvall's car hauler pulled up to the pit entrance next to us. The hauler was sporting the Flintstone Flyer logos and the name, Mike Duvall. The lady next to Big Larry turned to her husband and said in a country voice, "Mike Duvall, Mike Duvall ... Honey, you ever heard of Mike Duvall?" Big Larry turned and looked at me with an astonished look on his face and said to me, "I don't believe this." He then turned to the woman and said, "Don't worry. When he gets on the track you will most likely find out who he is." Well, Duvall went on to win the race over a good field of race cars, and I bet the lady and her husband knew who Mike Duvall was after that.

During his NDRA days Duvall won one of Smawley's biggest bonus incentives, the Lunati Cams $50,000 bonus, collected only if you won three NDRA races in a row. After winning, Mike was kind enough to give 10% of the bonus to a Christian fellowship group to help them build a new fellowship hall in Gaffney, SC. He also won the NDRA Championship in 1982. Mike has scored a number of major wins including the "super bowl" of dirt racing events; the 1982 World 100 at the famed Eldora Speedway at Rossburg, Ohio. In addition, he has won several $10,000 to win races such as, the

Stick Elliot Memorial numerous times, a STAR's race at Cherokee Speedway, three Hav-A-Tampa Dirt Series races, and 14 wins on the NDRA tour, as well as numerous wins all over the Southeast. In 2008, he won the super late model track championship in his final full season of racing at Cherokee Speedway, his home track. During a high point in his racing career he won $240,000 at Volusia, Florida in a week's worth of racing. In 2001 Mike Duvall was inducted into the National Dirt Late Model Hall of Fame in its first year.

Today, Mike Duvall teaches dirt late model racing at his Mike Duvall Racing School in Cowpens, South Carolina. Opened in 1993, it is one of the most popular driving schools in the country, graduating hundreds of drivers over the years. Duvall said he loves teaching almost as much as racing. During his racing days he always did most of the set-up work on his race car's himself. Mike now teaches this valuable racing knowledge to his many students at the racing school.

In a career that spanned five decades, Duvall won an amazing 1,026 feature races. His last win was in April 2010 at the Union County Speedway in Buffalo, S.C. Mike won a crate late model race in a Flintstone Flyer race car, holding off David Smith and Blake Bentley for the win. Duvall's son, Jonathan finished seventh in the event. I talked recently with Mike and I can tell he takes great pride in teaching his sons, Jonathan and Mitchell, what he knows about dirt late model racing. I feel sure we have another Flintstone Flyer just around the corner.

JODY RIDLEY

Chatsworth Georgia's Jody Ridley was born on May 9, 1942. Jody's accomplishments on the NASCAR Cup Series and his achievements on the asphalt short tracks are well known. Those include, 1980 NASCAR Winston Cup (now Sprint Cup) Rookie of the Year, 140 career Cup starts, 56 top ten finishes, and the 1981 Mason-Dixon 500 winner at Dover International Speedway. Other notable achievements on the asphalt short tracks were, seven NASCAR All-Pro Championships in the short track division, and

*Jody Ridley driving the Famous #98 blue and white Falcon. (Photo pro-
vided by Jody Ridley)*

the 1985 Snowball Derby winner. However, Ridley was among the
best dirt drivers to ever race the dirt tracks of the South. It is Jody
Ridley's dirt racing career that is the focus of his profile in chapter
five's "Dirt Warriors of the Past."

Jody started racing in 1965 at Boyd's Speedway in Chattanooga, Tennessee, and at the Cleveland Speedway, in nearby
Cleveland, Tennessee. Ridley became an instant crowd favorite
with the local race fans. This was due to his aggressive driving
style and the fact that he drove one of the few Ford race cars at
the time, the trademark blue and white 1956 Ford #98. After only
a couple of races he won his first race at the Cleveland Speedway. A few races later he scored his first of many feature wins at
Boyd's. Jody told me that during one period at Boyd's, "He won
13 races in a row."

During this early part of his racing career, Ridley began traveling to other tracks in the region such as, Sugar Creek Raceway in

Blue Ridge, Georgia; and the ½ mile Rome Speedway, which ran on Sunday afternoons. At the time Boyd's ran on Friday and Sunday nights, while Cleveland raced on Saturday nights and Rome ran a "matinee" racing program on Sunday afternoons. Jody was able to run sometimes four and even five times a week, which was not uncommon for drivers during this time.

Late in 1966 Jody built the legendary blue and white 1964 Ford Falcon. This was a dominant race car for years on both the dirt and asphalt short tracks throughout the South. One year I remember Ridley winning 61 feature races with that race car.

It was at this time that one of the funniest and most memorial events occurred during the time I spent around Jody. He had won the race on Friday night at Boyd's, then on Saturday night another feature win at Cleveland. The next day, Jody traveled down the road to the Rome Speedway and was leading the race over Joe Lee Johnson when he blew the engine in the Falcon. We were all dejected and sitting around the garage wishing we could race at Boyd's that night. Ralph, Jody's brother, had just recently bought a new turquoise and white Ford Bronco that happened to be sitting in front of the garage. Guess what, it had a 289 c.i. engine in it. I believe it was Biddle who called Ralph and asked if he could take the engine from the Bronco and put it in the race car. He got Ralph's permission and they quickly went to work putting the stock 289 engine in the Falcon. Jody said they only changed a few things on the engine, such as installing the headers and changing the carburetor. The race car was then loaded on the trailer and away they went to Boyd's in Chattanooga. The race was a close one between Jody and Friday Hassler in his #39 orange Chevy II, with Ridley taking the checkered flag for the win in a thrilling finish. A protest was lodged against Jody and his Falcon. A crowd gathered around as the engine was inspected by track officials and found to be a "stock 289." Most of the crowd was amused by the outcome. However, Hassler and his crew were clearly not pleased to have been out run by a stock Ford engine.

It was not long after Jody started racing that Ernie Elliott (Bill Elliott's brother), who operated Standard Speed Supply in

Dawsonville, Georgia, started building race engines for Jody's 1956 Ford. He also built them for the famous 1964 Falcon, and later for his 1968 Ford Fairlane. Jody and his brother Biddle were a successful team together, Jody handled the engine chores, while Biddle kept the car race ready, which included doing the paint and body work.

In the late 60's and into the early 70's, a number of tracks place "bounties" on drivers who were dominating at certain tracks. One of these tracks was the Hartwell Speedway, located in Hartwell, Georgia. A driver by the name of Rudy Burroughs was a constant winner at the track. He was sponsored by his dad's "Swamp Guinea" Restaurant and their slogan was, "Come pick a bone with us." Hartwell several times placed a bounty on Rudy. I recall Jody going to Hartwell a couple of times to try an win the bounty on the "Swamp Guinea," as we called him. However, neither of us could remember if he collected the bounty. However, Jody did mention he collected a bounty on Buck Simmons one time at Turner Speedway in Cummings, Georgia. One must remember, during this time there were no touring racing series and few track championships for drivers to earn extra money. So a number of drivers would search out tracks that had a bounty on a certain driver. Jody was one of those drivers and even had "The Bounty Hunter" on the front of the hood of his Ford Fairlane for a while.

Around 1968 Jody bought "Big Bertha," as we called her. The race car was a 1963 Ford NASCAR sportsman car that Ridley bought from Bob Wright. Jody ran the car several times, but it was at Lakewood Speedway in Atlanta late in 1968 that this memorable event occurred. If you remember the track had a first turn that was actually the first "corner" (a city street came up to this part of the track and it was cut into a corner to allow for the street). Race Cars had to go single file through this "corner." On this race day Jody and Joe Lee Johnson started on the pole, both driving 63 Fords. As the cars came down the long front straight-way under green, neither Jody or Joe Lee backed off and the result was both wrecked taking several rows of race cars behind them out also. However, track officials did stop the race and let everyone who could fix their cars.

In the early 70's Ridley went racing at the newly opened Dixie Speedway in Woodstock, Georgia. This was a "hornet's nest" of some of the best dirt drivers around at the time. Every Saturday night there were at least 10 or so drivers who had a legitimate shot to win the feature. Those included Buck Simmons, who dominated the track the first year, winning 18 of 22 races. Also on hand were, Leon Sells, Doug Kenimer, Charlie Mincey, and a number of others. Jody was driving a 68 Fairlane at Dixie (Falcon could not race here) and after a few races got his first win at the track. Jody said his first win at Dixie was one of his most memorable wins because he beat Buck and a lot of other good drivers, and did it in a Ford.

Between 1972 and 1976 Dixie Speedway was an asphalt track. During this "Asphalt Era," Jody Ridley won more races at Dixie than any other driver, a total of 46 features. In addition to winning against such local drivers as, Simmons, Mincey, and McGinnis; Ridley also won against some of NASCAR's best, beating the likes of Richard Petty, David Pearson, and Bobby Allison.

Jody continued to run the dirt tracks with the 64 Falcon late into the 70's. During Ridley's dirt racing career he raced at tracks all over the South. Those dirt tracks included, Lavonia Speedway in, Lavonia, GA., Atomic Speedway in Knoxville, TN., Holiday Downs Speedway in, Fairburn, GA., Toccoa Speedway in, Toccoa, GA., Senoia Speedway in Senoia, GA., Smoky Mountain Speedway in Maryville, TN., Gadsden Speedway in Gadsden, ALA., Gilmer County Speedway in Ellijay, GA., Canton International Speedway in Canton, GA., Cherokee Motor Speedway (Sutalee) in Waleska, GA., to name but a few of the many tracks Ridley competed on. He won the last race in the legendary blue and white 64 Falcon on the red clay of West Atlanta Raceway in late 1978. Ridley continued to race the clay ovals in the 80's. Jody drove a few dirt races for Russell Lee in the early 80's. In a bit of irony, Jody won his last dirt race at the Cleveland Speedway in 1985, driving a car owned by Lamar Clark. The irony being, he won both his first and last dirt races at the Cleveland Speedway in Cleveland, Tennessee.

During Jody's 39 year racing career he was perhaps one of the few drivers in racing who was a dominant force on both the dirt and asphalt shorts tracks throughout the country. Ridley won around 500 races on the short tracks during his career. Jody was inducted into the Georgia Racing Hall of Fame in Dawsonville, Georgia in 2007. Jody Ridley will always be remembered in the dirt racing circles as the driver of the blue and white #98 "Flying Ford Falcon."

"LITTLE" BILL CORUM

"Little" Bill Corum wins fast qualifier award at Atomic Speedway. (Photo courtesy of Little Bill)

"Little" Bill Corum was one of those racing Corums out of the Maynardville Tennessee area, that included "Big" Bill and Melvin Corum. "Little" Bill was born in Union County Tennessee in 1938. He began his racing career around 1960 and was a dominate force in Southern dirt racing for over 30 years.

Corum started racing the popular jalopies of the 50's and 60's at the Ashway Speedway. It was evident to anyone watching Little Bill that he had a natural talent for dirt racing. He won his first race in his very first start at the Ashway Speedway, driving a modified 37 Ford. Corum told me that the first race car he owned was a

1941 Ford that he and his father built from the ground up, and in the process almost burned down the building they were welding it together in. However, they did complete the race car and the building remained intact. Little Bill quickly graduated to late model racing and this is where he would race for the rest of his long and successful career.

Corum would go on to be one of the best dirt late model warriors that East Tennessee has ever produced. He raced dirt tracks all over East Tennessee, Kentucky, Georgia, and South Carolina. Some of the many dirt ovals he raced included, Atomic Speedway, Boyd's Speedway, Ashway Speedway, Anderson (SC) Speedway, Appalachian Speedway, Volunteer Speedway, Tazewell Speedway, and the Wartburg Speedway to name but a few. Little Bill had some success on the asphalt tracks like the Corbin (KY) Speedway, New Smyrna (FLA) Speedway, and the tiny asphalt track known as the Knoxville Raceway where he won the first three races at the track.

Little Bill told me that his two favorite tracks were, Atomic Speedway and Appalachian Speedway. He said he still liked Appalachian although he had one of the worst wrecks of his career at that track. It was during a feature race, Corum and Doug Kenimer had been racing side by side for about 13 laps and a race car ended up backwards in a blind spot in a turn. As both Kenimer and Little Bill came through the turn, Corum said he hit the car head on and was side lined for quite a while.

A lot of drivers during the 60's ran sometimes four and five times a week. Little Bill said, during one five day period he won an incredible four feature wins in four starts. Corum won Wednesday at a special race at Appalachian Speedway, traveled to North Georgia Speedway and won on Friday night; then came back to Atomic Speedway and won on Saturday night; then topped the weekend off with a win on the asphalt at the Corbin Speedway on Sunday. Corum said that was probably the best winning streak of his career. Little Bill said the most wins he had in a season was a 30 win season one year.

Corum ran a number of races in Robert Smawley's National Dirt Racing Association (NDRA) in the 80's, finishing in the top

five several times. He said his most memorable win came on November 8, 1981 at an NDRA race at Atomic Speedway. That day he
won the "Stroh's" 100 over an elite field of drivers that included, H.
E. Vineyard (Driving Rodney Combs car to 2nd place finish), Buck
Simmons, Mike Duvall (the Flintstone Flyer), "Black" Jack Boggs,
Leon Archer, and a number of others. Little Bill said the best race
he ever watched was an NDRA race at Rome Speedway on April
20,1980. Unfortunately, he had to watch this race from the side-
lines, after being involved in a wreck during a heat race. Corum
said, Bud Lunsford was having a bad day and had to start the 100
lap feature in 20th position. When the race went green Lunsford
fell even further back to 22nd position, but then Bud started to
move steadily through the field of NDRA stars. As the laps passed
Lunsford was passing cars at a fairly good clip, one or two cars
ever few laps or so. Little Bill said, "I turned to my wife and said, I
know who is going to win this race." She said, "Who?" and I said,
"Bud Lunsford," and my wife said, "No way, not against this field
of cars." As the race was winding down Lunsford moved into the
top five. Then Bud moved to second with a few laps to go. As the
white flag came out Lunsford caught Rodney Combs and was able
to pass him and win a close race at the checkered flag.

Corum said he bought most of his racing engines from Bowe
Laws, who ran a race engine shop in Orlando, Florida. Little Bill
said Laws provided some of the best race engines he ever ran. After
competing in the NDRA series, Little Bill Continued to race locally
at Atomic, Tazewell, Smoky Mountain, Volunteer, and other tracks
in the region. He won numerous races and several late model track
championships at tracks such as Atomic Speedway, Volunteer
Speedway, Tazewell Speedway, and the Newport Speedway. Corum was the driver for Butch Curtis for a number of races, and had
some classic battles with Scott Bloomquist while in the Curtis race
car. Little Bill said he ran his last late model dirt race at Smoky
Mountain Speedway in 1992. I asked Corum who his toughest
competitors were in racing, and he said, "Those Georgia boys were
tuff, especially Lunsford, Kenimer, Archer, and Simmons."

By his account, Corum won almost 400 feature wins during his 32 year career. He has been elected to a number of dirt

track Hall of Fame's they include, Atomic Speedway, 411 Speedway, Volunteer Speedway, Smoky Mountain Speedway, and the Tazewell Speedway. Little Bill Corum is an East Tennessee legend in late model dirt racing. If you are ever at the Tazewell Speedway, look around and you might just find him enjoying the races. Take a minute and talk racing with Little Bill, you will be glad you did.

LEON SELLS

Leon "Slick" Sells before a race at the Rome Speedway. (Photo provided by Leon Sells)

Leon Sells was born on April 14, 1936 in Lawrenceville, Georgia. Sells was known throughout his racing career as "Slick," a nickname his brother-in-law, Ed Massey gave him. I have known Leon since the early 70's and "Slick" best describes him. He would "Slick" his way through the competition, and be in the lead before you knew it. Sells and Massey would "Slick" the other race teams by playing mind games. They would do such things as, changing parts on their race engines to make them look different, or keep them guessing about how much the race car actually weighed. He was Leon "Slick" Sells one of the best Georgia dirt late model drivers to ever climb into race car.

Sells began his racing career around 1953 at the Old Canton Speedway. His first time in a race car was quite by accident, driving a 37 Ford Coupe when Curley Allison, the regular driver failed to show up. Leon said, "I got in the car and they showed me what to do, and as I was waiting for the green flag my knees were pattin' together like I was at a square dance." He went on to say, "Once the green flag came out, I was alright, and I was hooked from then on." Leon said a short time later that he and Ed Massey built their first race car, a 34 Ford, and ran it in several races throughout the region.

Later, Coley Avery, from Cummings, Georgia, brought a wrecked "skeeter" race car by the shop and wanted Leon and Ed to repair it. He said he would let Sells drive the car for fixing it. Avery was more interested in collecting "tow money" (money tracks paid out for race cars to be brought to the track) than being competitive or winning. Avery always wanted Leon "to take it easy" on the engine and not try to win the race. Soon Sells grew tired of this and one night at Boyd's Speedway in Chattanooga, he decided to try and go for the lead. Well the engine gave up and Avery was dejected. However, the next night Leon and Ed were at Atlanta's Peach Bowl Speedway, walking around in the pits, when who came through the pit gate? It was Avery with the race car in tow. Leon and Ed walked over and asked him where he got an engine and how did he get it in the car that quick. Coley called them aside and said in a low voice, "Be quite; its the same blown engine. I'm gonna tell them something happened and I can't run and get the tow money."

After that adventure Ed and Leon bought a skeeter from C.P. Shaw. It was the same one Charlie Mincey had driven to a number of wins for Shaw. Leon had a lot of success with the car before building his first late model, a 1955 Chevy. Later, Massey and

Sells would build identical '55 Chevys and hire Charlie Mincey to drive the second race car. They would take the cars to different tracks to try and win as many races and as much money as possible. Leon would race the tracks North of Atlanta, while Mincey would race South of Atlanta. Sells has driven a number of different types of race cars during his long career. Among them were, Chevy Chevelles, Novas, Camaros, and even a Ford Mustang at one time.

Leon said he never kept up with how many races he won. Sells said, "When a race was over no matter if I won or not, that race was behind me, and I was focusing on the next race." Leon has won races all over the South; from Boyd's Speedway, in Chattanooga, TN; to many other tracks like West Atlanta, Senoia, Dixie Speedway, Rome Speedway, the Peach Bowl, Jeffco, Middle Georgia, and many others. His favorite track was the old Lakewood Speedway where he posted a number of memorable win, the first was in his '55 Chevy. In the early '70's Sells also won races at a couple of tracks you never hear much about, Holiday Downs in Fairburn, Georgia, and the Chickamauga Raceway in Chickamauga, Georgia. Chickamauga was a motorcycle track and Leon and Buck Simmons had a classic battle there with Sells coming out the winner in the first and only race held at the track.

Leon said some of the toughest competition was at Rome, Dixie and West Atlanta in the '70's when such driver as Doug Kenimer, Buck Simmons, Charlie Bagwell, Jody Ridley, Luther Carter, Charlie Mincey, and others were running. Sells said every night any of these drivers were capable of winning. Although the exact number of wins that Leon accumulated over his long career will never be known. One thing is for certain, when he climbed into the #77 for the last time at Dixie Speedway in 1988, his win total was in the several hundreds range.

Leon "Slick" Sells was inducted into the Georgia Racing Hall of Fame in 2009. Leon will receive the ultimate honor for any dirt late model driver in August of 2015, when he is inducted into the National Dirt Late Model Hall of Fame, in Florence, Kentucky.

H. E. VINEYARD

H. E. Vineyard takes another win at Atomic Speedway in the Miller Bros.
#3. (Photo provided by H. E. Vineyard and "Peanut" Jenkins)

H. E. (Doc) Vineyard was born in Knoxville, Tennessee on January 8, 1938. Vineyard is from the old school of dirt racing. During the 60's and most of the 70's, most of the successful drivers built and worked on their own race cars, he was one of those drivers. I have known Vineyard since the mid-70's and one thing I can say about H. E., he was one of the hardest racing dirt late model drivers that ever raced the red clay ovals of the South. During the time I worked in the pits with his crew chief David "Peanut" Jenkins in the mid-80's; what I remember most about H. E. was his never give up attitude on a race or his race car. Vineyard always said, "Whatever it takes to win."

Vineyard started racing around 1959 at Ashway Speedway in Strawberry Plains, TN. Not long afterwards, his first win came at Edgemoore Speedway, a tiny asphalt track that was located Oak in Ridge, TN. He has also raced asphalt at the old Knoxville Raceway and the Corbin Speedway in Kentucky. During Vineyard's long career he raced at tracks all over the Southeast, from Florida, Georgia, Tennessee, and Kentucky.

Vineyard competed in the Knoxville and surrounding areas at tracks like the Tazewell Speedway throughout much of his early career. In the mid to late 70's, as tracks like Volunteer Speedway at Bull's Gap, TN., and Atomic Speedway near Knoxville, TN. started to open, H. E. began running and winning often at these tracks. For example, the 1979 July 4th weekend was perhaps the biggest racing weekend of his career. Vineyard went 4 for 4; on June 29th he won a 40 lap race at Volunteer; the next night he won a 100 lapper at Atomic; that was followed up on July 1st by another win at Volunteer; then two days later he won a 150 lap race back at Atomic.

Around 1979, H.E. was introduced to Bob Boyce, a fabricator and chassis builder from Mel-Rose Park, ILL. Boyce built Vineyard a racing chassis known as the "Track Burner." H.E. had a lot of success using this chassis in race cars during the '79 and '80 racing seasons, winning a career high 41 feature races in 1979. One of those wins was the biggest and most memorable win of H.E. Vineyard's career. It was the National Dirt Racing Association (NDRA) race at Volunteer Speedway on June 9,1979. He beat Buck Simmons by a half-car-length at the finish line in the $30,000 Looney Cheverolet 100.

Vineyard raced in Kentucky quite a bit while driving for Bob Miller (Miller Bros. Construction Co. and Hawkeye Trucking Co.) and Speck Parsons (P and P Wrecking Yard), during the 80's. One track he was almost unbeatable at was Rock Castle County Speedway, located in Mount Vernon, KY. Vineyard had several wins and track championships over the years there, beating the likes of John Gill, Randy Boggs, "Black" Jack Boggs and several others. The first time I made the trip to Rock Castle with Vineyard I thought I was on a movie set. If the movie, WE BOUGHT A ZOO, had been released at the time, that movie set would fit this speedway perfectly. There was a petting zoo, a caged bear, plenty of chickens, and an old barn in the pits. In fact during qualifying, H.E. hit a big rooster going down the back straight-away, and boy did the feathers fly. Although the rooster never made it, Vineyard did go on to win the pole and the race that night.

In the 1980's, at a UMP race at Rock Castle, Vineyard and John Gill had been in a close racing battle for the lead most of the night. Vineyard said, "On the last lap Gill, racing the high groove, got beside a lapped car racing the low groove, thinking this would keep me behind him. However, as we headed toward the finish line, I hit the lapped car very hard in the rear end, knocking it forward. This enabled me to pass Gill and beat him at the finish line by about two feet."

Another track Vineyard enjoyed great success while driving the white #3 dirt late model for Miller and Parsons was Atomic Speedway near West Knoxville, Tennessee. Vineyard dominated the track not only in the late model class, but also the 9 to 1 class. He had several winning streaks in both classes during his run in the #3. He won track championships in '79, '81, and '87. He was also elected to Atomic's Hall of Fame in 1995.

In 1986, at a race at Barren County (KY) Speedway, you get a glimpse of just how strong Vineyard's will to win was. The night before, at Taylor County (KY) Speedway, H.E. was involved in a wreck that bent the frame of his race car. The race team worked most of the night straightening the frame. The next day at Barren County, they not only were able to race; but won the race beating, Jeff Purvis, Randy Boggs, Fats Coffey, and Jack Boggs. In 1986 came another big win, the 9 to 1 class Tennessee Dirt Track Championship at Atomic. In this race Scott Bloomquist led 99 laps, but was passed by Vineyard on the last lap for the win. In 1987 H.E. added another big win to his resume at Atomic, the late model Tennessee Dirt Track Championship. Vineyard continued to win races during the '90's racing Masterbuilt, C. J. Rayburn, Rocket, as well as other racing chassis. Vineyard made the famed World 100 field of 24 six times ('76, '77, '79, '85, '86, and '87). His best finish in the legendary race was a 7th in 1986.

Vineyard ran his last official race at Volunteer Speedway at Bull's Gap, TN. In 2002. In true "Doc" Vineyard form, he won the race. However, at a 2008 legends race at Smoky Mountain Speedway, Vineyard raced his nephew, Mark Vineyard's, car and ran off and left the field in the "Buddy Rogers Memorial Race." According to some who saw the race, he was actually turning laps faster than Dale McDowell, who had won the super late model race that day. After visiting and talking with H. E. the other day, I told him, "I think you need to get a race car and let's go racing." I have no doubt he could still do it.

H.E. Vineyard was inducted into the National Dirt Late model Hall of Fame in 2007. He is without a doubt, one of the best late model dirt drivers to ever come out of the Volunteer State.

CHARLES HUGHES

Charles Hughes' #39 Southeastern Latex Sales Late model. (Photo provided by Charles Hughes)

Charles Hughes was born in Bradley County, Tennessee, on March 16, 1941. This is only about a short thirty minute drive from his current home in Dalton, Georgia. I first met Charles when we were both helping Jody Ridley at his race shop and as part of his early pit crew in the mid-60's. Biddle, Jody's brother, was the mainstay of the crew; doing most of the body work, painting, and helping with race car set-ups. In 1966, Biddle decided to try his hand at racing, and together with Hughes, built their first race car together. The '56 Ford #9 was a co-driver affair. Charles would drive the car one night and Biddle the next. The car even had both their names on the top. This co-driver operation last about a year and Biddle bought Hughes' part of the car. Charles then bought a '55 Chevy late model from Leon Brindle, a long time late model driver himself. This was Charles' first car of his own. Hughes raced the #3 Chevy at North Georgia Speedway and at the Cleveland (TN) Speedway. Charles told me recently, "Over the years a lot of people have asked me how I arrived at my racing number 39 which I ran almost my whole career. It was easy for me. I just took the numbers of my first two race cars and reversed them, thus #39."

In 1968, Charles started driving for Dalton's Lamar Kyle. Hughes drove a '67 slop backed Ford mustang to a number of wins at Cleveland, Rome, and at the old Gilmer County Speedway in Ellijay, GA.

Around 1970, Hughes started driving for E. D. Ridley, Jr. Charles won a number of races throughout the region over the next few years. It was while driving for Ridley that Charles' fortunes were about to go national. In early 1976, Hughes purchased a new "radically" designed racing chassis from a new company in Phenix City, Alabama. The company was called Jig-A-Lo Racing Chassis. This turned out to be one of the best decisions Charles made during his entire racing career. During the '76 season Hughes, driving a Chevy Camaro with the new Jig-A-Lo chassis, won 43 races. A number of these were high paying races; like the U. S. National 100 at Champaign, Illinois; and East Alabama Motor Speedway's National 100. However, none could compare to his winning the 1976 World 100 at the famed Eldora Speedway. He won the race over fellow Georgia driver, Doug Kenimer, who was also racing a Jig-A-Lo chassis. Also, in '76 Hughes was the State Late Model Champion in four different states. Those states were, Alabama, Georgia, Tennessee, and North Carolina.

On a later trip to Eldora, Charles told me a funny incident that happened. Hughes was having engine problems, and had to change engines at the track. He had been running and winning with a small three disc, light weight racing clutch. After removing it and placing it beside the trailer where they were working. He wrapped it in a towel. He wanted to keep the other drivers from knowing the type of clutch he was using. Charles said, "As I was hurriedly replacing the engine, a noisy fellow driver, Billy Clanton, had unwrapped the towel and saw the clutch." Hughes said, "By the time I got back home everyone was using this clutch."

In 1977, Charles was about to drive for the last car owner he would ever drive for. Hughes teamed with Billy Cady, owner of Southeastern Latex Sales. This turned out to be a winning combination. During the NDRA days of the early '80's, Charles drove a Baird & Trivette race car. The Atlanta based company built two cars for the Cady-Hughes team. They specialized in road course race cars. However, they did build a few top notch race cars for the dirt tracks. Another car they built was the one Leon Archer had great success driving on the NDRA circuit; until it was stolen during an NDRA event at Atomic Speedway. Over the next twenty years, the Cady-Hughes team would win around 500 races all over the Southeast. At such tracks as, Tri-County (NC) Speedway, North Georgia Speedway, Boyd's Speedway, Dixie Speedway, Rome Speedway, Lavonia Speedway, Hartwell Speedway,Toccoa Speedway, West Atlanta Raceway, and Senoia Speedway, to name but a few of the many tracks they won on. Sadly, in 1997 Billy Cady passed away and Charles retired from racing; but not before winning the '97 North Georgia Speedway Track Championship.

During Charles Hughes' long career he got the checkered flag for over 750 feature wins. Charles was inducted into the National Dirt Late Model Hall of Fame in 2005.

FREDDY SMITH

The Tar Heel State's Freddy Smith was born in Kings Mountain, North Carolina on December 22, 1946. Smith grew up around the world of automobile racing. His father, Clarence "Grassy"

Freddy Smith's crew works quickly to get the #00 ready for the 100 lap feature at Atomic. (Photo provided by Nick Nicholson)

Smith ran a race shop that built race engines for one of NASCAR's pioneer Ford race car builders, Holman Moody. Freddy's racing career began as an 8 year old, racing go-karts. However, by 1966 he was racing stock cars. During his early career, Smith raced mainly in the North Carolina area. He also made frequent trips to one of his favorite tracks, Gaffney South Carolina's, Cherokee Speedway. The Starlite Speedway, located near Hudson, North Carolina, was the site of a lot of Freddy's early late model wins.

The first time I saw Smith race was, during Robert Smawley's NDRA series in 1980. It was at the Volunteer Speedway in Bulls Gap, TN. Freddy had been on a hot streak during the year, having all ready won four NDRA races. He was hoping to win the year's final series race. Smith did go on to score the victory at "The Gap," giving him five wins for the season. This was by far the most wins by a driver in a season for the dirt late model series' young history. That successful NDRA season landed Freddy's racing team their first major sponsor. Beady Lynch, an avid race fan, was also president of B & D Industrial Boilers in North Charleston, SC. He agreed to sponsor Smith for the '81 NDRA season. After a poor showing at Florida's Volusia County Speedway, going through four engines in three days. Freddy's team turned things around with wins in a 75 lap race at the Oglethorpe Speedway and a 100 lap event at Savannah Speedway.

Freddy Smith is one of the few drivers that I have watched compete in a number of late model dirt series throughout most of his career. I saw him win two of his nine NDRA series wins, one at the Volunteer Speedway ('80) and the other at the Kingsport Speedway ('85); I also witnessed him take 4 of his 19 checkered flags in the Hav-A-Tampa series, three at Cherokee (SC) Speedway ('94, '95, '97) and a win at North Georgia Speedway ('96). Later, I saw Freddy score victories in the Southern All-Stars Dirt Racing Series at Thunder Valley Speedway in Lawndale, NC (2001 and 2002). From '99 until '02 Freddy dominated Southern All-Star races at Thunder Valley, winning five of his seven series wins at that track.

A few of Freddy's 784 career wins include major wins in the late model dirt racing world. They include, three Blue/Gray 100 wins ('91, 2000, and '01) at Cherokee (SC) Speedway; five Dirt Track World Championships ('83, '85,'91, '93, and '98); two Hillbilly 100's ('81, and '83); and finally, a two time winner of Eldora Speedway's "The Dream" ('94 and 2000). However, the "Southern Gentleman" was a long way from being finished with big wins. On July 11, 2008, Freddy Smith, at age 61, won his first Lucas Oil Late Model Dirt Series race at North Alabama Speedway in Tuscumbia, Alabama.

Freddy Smith raced the nations dirt tracks for 48 years, hanging up his racing helmet in 2012. Smith will always be remembered as the driver of the legendary red, white, and blue # 00 dirt late model. Smith was inducted into The National Dirt Late Model Hall of Fame in its inaugural class in 2001.

CHAPTER SIX:

THE DIRT WARRIORS OF TODAY

In the final chapter we take a look at some of today's super late model dirt warriors. A few of these drivers are in the twilight of their racing careers, having already achieved success on the national level. Some are already in the National Dirt Late Model Hall of Fame. Others are still gaining their fame and success as they enter the midpoint of their super late model careers. Many are the young guns of today's super late model dirt battles. The up and coming stars who will write their own chapter in the history of super late model dirt racing.

SCOTT BLOOMQUIST

Scott Bloomquist after Qualifying for Lucas Oil race at Smoky Mountain Speedway in 2015. (Photo provided by the author)

Scott Bloomquist is arguable the most innovative and successful super late model driver to race the nation's dirt tracks over the last 30 years. Winning is what he does best and, at the age of 51, I don't see him slowing down anytime soon. The first time I saw Scott was at the Atomic Speedway in Knoxville, Tennessee in 1986. He was the "California Kid," who had moved to the South and was winning big at a number of East Tennessee dirt tracks. He was fresh off his dominating season at the Kingsport Speedway in 1984. The next two years found Bloomquist winning races all over the Knoxville area at tracks like, Tazewell, Atomic, Smoky Mountain, and even the Volunteer Speedway at Bull's Gap, Tennessee. In 1986 Bloomquist had one of his best seasons, winning 35 of 45 races.

In the spring of 1986, it had been a rainy week in the Knoxville area and on Saturday night of that weekend at Atomic Speedway, the track was "sticking like glue." As qualifying began at the high banked 1/3 mile clay oval, Gary Hall qualified and broke the existing 1/3 mile world record. Not long after that record lap, H.E. Vineyard set yet another world record. A few minutes later young Bloomquist blistered the track in his #18 Katch One race car, setting yet another new record (at the time) of 11.29. That night I knew I had not only witnessed a world record being broken, but a new and different type of driver, one that would rise to the forefront of late model dirt racing for years to come.

Scott Bloomquist was born in Fort Dodge, Iowa on November 14, 1963. Scott's father, an airline pilot for Air California, moved the family to California where young Scott was raised. His dad was invited to watch a friend and also coworker race; the elder Bloomquist liked the race so much he bought a race car and decided to try the sport himself. After a short time behind the wheel, he decided racing was not for him and gave the car to his son. Scott's first race was at Corona Speedway in Corona, California in 1980. Racing at the track for a couple of years; Bloomquist won a number of races and the Track Championship in 1982.

In 1983, Scott heard that a track in Chula Vista, California was paying $4,000 to win the feature race. Bloomquist was about to become not only a good race driver, but also a race car and chassis builder as well. At the time, back East, it was the "wedge car" era in late model dirt racing. During this time, Bloomquist had seen a picture of the wedge car Charlie Swartz had raced to win the 1982 Dirt Track World Championship at the Pennsboro Speedway. So he decided to build a wedge car of his own. Scott showed up at Chula Vista Speedway with his radically designed race car and won the race, lapping the field twice in the process. After the race Scott's dad wanted to sell the car. However, Bloomquist worked out a deal to pay for the car by working on his father's new farm in Mooresburg, Tennessee. Young Bloomquist began to think of racing as a career.

In large part, the move to the South was made to get Scott near the center of dirt racing at the time; Kingsport, Tennessee and Robert Smawley's new NDRA series. Unfortunately for Scott, the NDRA was history after the 1985 season. Soon Bloomquist purchased a Barry Wright race car and started running in a number of high paying races. His first $10,000 win came at Isom, Kentucky. After several wins over the next few years, Bloomquist decided to try his hand at Eldora's famed World 100 in 1988. Bloomquist was immediately pitted against, three time World 100 winner, and racing legend at the time, Jeff Purvis. Scott started seventh in the race, almost unheard of for a rookie. Once the race went green Purvis took the lead from the start. However, Bloomquist slowly caught the leader and passed him for his first World 100 Win. Even after the win, Scott had to prove himself to the racing world. It took winning the pole the next year; followed by another World 100 win in 1990, to prove once and for all that he was one of the top Late model drivers in the country.

During the years from 1993 to 1996, Bloomquist raced the Hav-A-Tampa Dirt Racing Series, winning the series championship in both '94 and '95. He had an amazing 60 wins during that period, over three times as many as the second place driver with 18.

The 90's saw a number of notable wins in high profile events including; the '93 and '95 Pittsburgher; the Eldora Dream in '95; the Knoxville Late Model Nationals in '95; the Show-Me 100 in '95; and the National 100 at East Alabama Motor Speedway in '90, '93, '94, '97, and '99.

Bloomquist continued his winning ways in the 2000's, winning a number of big money events including; Five more Eldora Dreams in '02, '04, '06, '08, and '13; two more World 100's in 2000 and '14; three more National 100's in '01, '02, and '03; and four more Show-Me 100's in '03, '04, '05, and '08. In 2003, Scott competed in the Xtreme Dirt Car Series, winning a fifth over all Championship. In 2004 he won yet another national series championship, the World of Outlaws Late Model Series.

Although Bloomquist has won his share of series championships he never liked running for points in a series. Scott once said, "I think a racer should be able to pick and choose where he wants to race." Bloomquist likes going to high profile races with the stiff competition that is always found there. He once said, "That's what I live for." After running "outlaw" for a few years winning such races as; the '06 Topless 100; the '06 Dixie Shootout; and the '06 Racefest. Scott made the decision to return to series racing in 2009. Upon his return, he promptly won two Lucas Oil Late Model Dirt Series Championships in, '09 and 2010. Today, Bloomquist continues to run the Lucas Oil series. However, he is always looking for high profile, big money events to try and pull off a win. Scott's career winning percentage is in the mid-thirty range; and that is amazing when you take into consideration that he rarely runs a race that pays under $10,000. Another statistic than stands out even more, is his 70% winning percentage for first time visits to a race track.

As I said earlier, Scott Bloomquist is an innovator in chassis and car setups. Throughout his racing career he has worked on his own race cars. After racing chassis built by other Major companies; and having to modify them with innovations he has learned over decades of racing; he decided to build his own racing Chassis. Scott introduced the "Bloomquist Chassis,"in the early 2000's. At first only himself and a select few other drivers used his racing chassis. Among the first were; "The Newport Nightmare," Jimmy Owens; Gray Court, South Carolina's Chris Madden; and long time super late model driver Rick Eckert. Today, Scott along with Michigan racer and businessman, Randy Sweet have decided to halt sales for a while of the "Bloomquist Chassis" (Team Zero) to outside race teams. Their focus will be on building cars for Scott Bloomquist Racing.

After racing engines for a number of engine builders; like Somerset, Kentucky's Cornett Racing Engines; and Mosheim, Tennessee's Vic Hill Race Engines; Bloomquist signed on with Mooresville, North Carolina's Roush Yates Racing in 2010. Scott saw immediate results, winning several big events, and the 2010 Lucas Oil Dirt Late Model Championship. Today, Scott continues to have great success with their engine program, winning the 2014 DIRTCar Nationals Late Model points title at Volusia (FLA) Speedway Park, using the new Roush Yates 45. He also tests and sells Team Zero performance products through Roush Yates.

Finally, Bloomquist secured another major sponsor for 2015. This year NASCAR legend Mark Martin is teaming with Scott Bloomquist Racing. Mark Martin Automotive will sponsor Scott for a run at the 2015 Lucas Oil Dirt Late Model Championship.

Scott Bloomquist has over 550 wins to his credit. Most are hard earned high profile, big money wins. He has already been inducted into the National Dirt Late Model Hall of Fame in 2002. Since that Spring Saturday Night at Atomic Speedway in 1986; Scott has gone on to be the driver and the innovative car builder I knew he would. That look of determination I saw in young Bloomquist's eyes that night in '86 said it all. It said to me, "I have the will to succeed in the tough world of late model dirt."

JIMMY OWENS

Newport Tennessee's Jimmy Owens was born on February 3, 1972. The "Newport Nightmare," as he is known by race fans and drivers alike; came to the super late model ranks through a different path than most of today's dirt warriors. In 1991 Owens started briefly in the street stocks, racing for four years, winning his very first race at Kingsport (TN) Speedway and 56 other street wins along the way. He ran a few late model races in 1994, finishing, at the time, his career best fourth at Volunteer Speedway at Bulls Gap, TN.

Jimmy Owens the "Newport Nightmare" in the #20. (Photo provided by the author)

However, Owens was about to make a dramatic change in his choice of racing machines. Jimmy started running UMP modifieds in 1995. His inaugural season was very successful, winning 20 races along with a third place finish in the UMP points. In 1996 Owens teamed with car owner Danny Anders and he continued his winning ways in the modifieds. The next two years Jimmy took a total of 66 checkered flags in the UMP series. The highlight of the '98' season was the winning of his first UMP National Championship. During Owens' UMP modified career he has won four National titles (1998, 2000, 2001, and 2002). In 2001 he had a season most drivers only dream of. That year he won an amazing 49 modified features in 62 races. This would have been a racing career for some drivers, but not for the Owens. He was about to embark upon yet another racing career. That career was the big time world of super late model dirt racing.

In 2001 car owner Jerry Weisgarber steered Jimmy ever closer to a dirt late model career, having Owens drive in several races for him. Jimmy admitted it was a learning process. The super late models differed from the modifieds in two major areas, race suspensions (swing arm vs. four bar) and speed difference. In 2003 Owens decided to become a full-time race driver. Racing about half in modifieds and the other half in super late models. His best SLM finish was a win at the super fast Tazewell (TN) Speedway, winning a $10,000 payday.

However, 04' and '05 were somewhat disappointing seasons. Owens made the field for the famed World 100 both years, but unfortunately fell out of the two events. While leading in 04' with only 20 laps remaining Jimmy had a flat tire. The next year Owens had set a new track record and was running a strong sixth, when he was taken out in a wreck. There were some bright moments to go along with those disappointments. Driving for Mach 2 Motorsports Jimmy won 12 races in 2004 and won the Jani-King Southern Showdown and its $26,000 payout in 2005.

Jimmy Owens became a major force in super late model racing in 2007. Any doubts about his SLM ability was put to rest after he won the World 100 at the legendary Eldora Speedway in September, driving his Reece Monuments #20. It was truly a breakout season for Owens, winning the North/South 100 at the Florence (KY) Speedway; Cherokee (SC) Speedway's Blue/Gray 100; and the Racefest World Championship in Mineral Wells, VA. The 2007 season saw Owens win 17 Feature races. Most of these were big money races.

2008 was a very productive year for Jimmy as he won 14 super late model features, including the Tyler County(WV) Speedway's $40,000 Hillbilly 100 and five other $10,000 to win races. In 2009 he continued to capture big money races like no one since Kentucky's "Black" Jack Boggs during his brilliant career. He won the 15th Annual Dirt Late Model Dream at Eldora Speedway and its $100,000 prize. In another high profile race, Owens won the 17th Annual Comp Cams Topless 100 at Batesville (AR) Speedway and pocketed another $42,000.

Owens for many years had raced as an "Outlaw" racer (a driver who travels to big money or crown jewel races). This is the road

Scott Bloomquist has also taken many times over the years. On the heels of a very productive year in 2010; winning his second North/South 100; two World of Outlaws races; and eight Lucas Oil Late model Dirt Series wins; Jimmy decided to run the entire Lucas Oil Series in 2011. This proved to be a very good decision, as he won the Lucas Oil Late Model Dirt Series Championship in 2011, 2012, and 2013 for a three peat. Only Jacksonville Florida's Earl Pearson Jr. has more, winning four in a row earlier in the series.

In 2013 Owens had ten super late model victories, including the $20,000 Cotton Pickin 100 at the Magnolia (MS) Motor Speedway. 2014 saw Jimmy win 15 super late model races, including; a $50,000 payday at the USA Nationals at Cedar Lake (WI) Speedway. He also won another Topless 100 worth $40,000. Owens was second in 2014 Lucas Oil Series points to Martinsville Indiana's Don O'Neal, losing by only 65 points.

In 2015 Jimmy Owens is teaming with Brian Rowland Racing and Club 29 race cars out of Woodward, Oklahoma. Widow Wax will be the primary sponsor on the #20. Owens is one of the dominate drivers in today's super late model ranks. Jimmy displays that patient; never get upset attitude needed to be a winner in super late model racing. I observed this attitude in the two races I have seen him compete in during the 2015 season. The first was at Tazewell (TN) Speedway on April 12, at the World of Outlaws Late Model Series race. Starting in sixth position, Owens moved into the top three and patiently waited for the leader Josh Richards or Billy Ogle, Jr., running second, to make a mistake. On the final lap Richards was forced high by Ogles in turns three and four. As Richards, Ogles, and Owens were coming off turn four, Ogles passed Richards for the $10,000 win, taking Owens with him for second place.

The other race was at Maryville Tennessee's Smoky Mountain Speedway. It was the Old Man's Garage Spring Nationals on April 26. Jimmy had blown an engine in an earlier race while qualifying at Smokey Mountain and was unable to compete in that race. Owens was hoping for better results in the Old Man's Garage Race. However, during hot laps he again had engine woes; not getting upset Jimmy switched to a backup car and won his consolation race. In the 50 lap feature he rolled off from the fifth starting spot. He made a late race rally to nab the runner up spot to Casey Roberts at the finish. Patients and the never get upset attitude, helped Owens gain those two second place finishes. Jimmy Owens is a driver who likes to work on his own race cars and understands the workings of a race car. If you look around, all good drivers tend to work on their own cars. Jimmy Owens is one of those good drivers who runs well in the fast paced world of super late model racing.

JONATHAN DAVENPORT

Jonathan Davenport stands beside his car after hot laps at a Lucas Oil race. (Photo provided by the author)

The Peach State's Jonathan Davenport was born on October 31, 1983 in the Georgia mountain town of Blairsville, Georgia. Jonathan is another of the young guns of super late model dirt racing who started their careers racing go-karts. Davenport started kart racing in the junior classes, but quickly graduated to the adult classes well before his sixteenth birthday. From go-karts as a young kid, in the early '90's ; to the top of the Lucas Oil Late Model Dirt

Series standings in 2015, Jonathan's nickname of "Super Man" is starting to fit.

Davenport entered the world of stock car racing during his mid-teens, racing mini-stocks at Tri-County Speedway in Brasstown, NC. After winning the Mini-Stock Points Championships in '95 and '96, Jonathan started traveling to neighboring tracks in the area. He had a total of 30 career wins in mini-stock . After leaving the mini-stock ranks, Davenport focused on several other racing series. Those included; the Dixie Region Sem-Pro Series, winning the series point title in '99, along with 14 wins. He also won the Winter Series at Lanier (GA) National Speedway, scoring five wins in the process. In addition, he was the first to score back to back wins in The Young Lions National Championship, held at Texas Motor Speedway, winning in both '99 and 2000. Jonathan's attention then turned to legends racing, winning the '01 World Finals Legends Championship, and its richest ever first prize of $15,000. During his Legends Car Series career he was victorious a total of 104 times, the second most wins in the series by a driver to date.

In 2002 Davenport's interests shifted to super late model dirt racing. The young driver competed locally at such tracks as, Lavonia (GA) Speedway, and Ray Cook's Tri-County (NC) Speedway. He also raced at, what he calls his home track, the legendary Toccoa (GA) Speedway. 2004 proved to be a good year he scored a number of wins, including, winning the "Topless 40", along with 10 other wins that year. In 2005 he ventured Into touring series racing, with the Southern All-Stars Dirt Racing Series. Jonathan scored his first SAS win at the Cleveland (TN) Speedway in the "Joe Lee Johnson Memorial."

Davenport signed on as a driver for Gaffney South Carolina's Hamrick Motorsports in '06. He ran in the Carolina Clash Late Model Series, winning a series race at Laurens (SC) Speedway. He also scored a victory in the "Modoc 50" at Modoc (SC) Speedway, along with eight other checkered flags. After a good season with Hamrick, Jonathan started driving for the Mark Beaver Motorsports team in'07. It was with this race team that Davenport scored his first $10,000 win. He also won the track Championship at the old Thunder Valley (NC) Speedway that same year.

2008 was a busy year for the young Blairsville native, winning races in several different touring series. Davenport picked up a win on the Southern All-Stars tour at Lavonia (GA) Speedway; two Carolina Clash super late model wins at Wythe Raceway in Rural Retreat, Virginia; two victories in the Carolina Clash crate late model division; and finally, two Fastrak Crate Late Model Series checkered flags. All total, Jonathan had 16 wins for the season.

The 2009 season was perhaps the turning point in Davenport's career. He signed on with, not one, but two racing teams. He decided to race crate late models for Craig Patterson racing in the #49 car. He made one of the best decisions of his career, by joining forces with Kevin Rumley at K&L Racing to drive super late models. He drove a Barry Wright house car #6 for the famed Cowpens, South Carolina chassis builder. He immediately had success with both race teams, winning the Fastrak series Modoc 100, and three Fastrak Spring Tour races in three days for the Patterson Team. He also had a good season in Rumley's super late model, winning the annual March Madness race at Cherokee Speedway in Gaffney, SC; the Shrine 100 at Carolina Speedway in Gastonia, NC; and the big National 100 race at East Alabama Motor Speedway in Phenix City, Alabama.

A lot of big money wins were in store for Davenport and his dual race teams in 2010. He won the $25,000 Crate Nationals title at Green Valley (ALA) Speedway; two $10,000 Fastrak Crate late model Series wins. Then in Rumley's super late model he scored victories at the Cleveland (TN) Speedway's $10,000 annual Shamrock Race; and was the winner of two $10,000 Lucas Oil Series races. In 2011, he continued to see a number of big event wins. Those victories included, Cherokee (SC) Speedway's Blue/Gray 100, and the Cotton Pickin 100 at the legendary Magnolia (MS) Motor Speedway. However, 2012 proved to be some what of an off year for Davenport. He did win two $10,000 unsanctioned super late model races. Jonathan also continued to collect wins on the Fastrak Crate Late Model Series with a $5,000 win. The bright spot for the 2012 season, was winning the Lucas Oil Late Model Dirt Series Rookie of the Year honors.

2013 was a good year for Davenport and Rumley's super late model race team. They captured the Schaeffer Oil Southern Nationals point title. The Team also scored a big victory in the $30,000 Carolina Crown race at Lancaster (SC) Speedway. Also, Jonathan had two wins on the Southern All-Star Dirt racing Series, winning at Smoky Mountain (TN) Speedway; and at the East Alabama Motor Speedway in Phenix City, Alabama. According to Davenport, East Alabama Motor Speedway is one of his favorite tracks. I can see why, Jonathan has scored three National 100 wins ('09, '11, and '14) and has been in victory lane on several other occasions. During 2013 Davenport also signed with Steve Cooke's AES Racing out of Mount Airy, North Carolina.

With Kevin Rumley now working with Longhorn Racing Chassis as chief engineer since 2012; it was only a matter of time until Jonathan would be racing on a Longhorn chassis. The K&L Race team started 2014 off with a bang, winning the Lucas Oil Late model Dirt Series race at Brunswick Georgia's Golden Isles Speedway in February. This was followed by a $10,000 win at Cherokee (SC) Speedway. Then he won his third National 100 at East Alabama Motor Speedway. In addition, he had several Fastrak Series wins; and a final Lucas Oil Late Model series win at Knoxville (IA) Raceway.

The current Lucas Oil Late Model Dirt Series season looks very promising for the K&L Race team. They have started off with a win in the Buckeye 50 at Atomic (OH) Speedway. The Longhorn chassis of the #6 super late model was working well at the Tazewell Speedway on May 30th of this year. I was at the super fast "Taz" to witness the Lucas Oil boys do battle. Scott Bloomquist appeared to have everything under control. He had the fast time and was leading the race through about lap 35 or so. Scott and the other racers were making the middle and low grooves work; but Davenport was finally able to make the high groove work and promptly went by Bloomquist for the $10,000 win.

The very next night at the Florence Speedway in Kentucky the results were the same. This time Jonathan led all 50 laps on his way to his second consecutive Lucas Oil win in two nights. It was Earl Pearson Jr. in another Longhorn chassis race car that passed

Bloomquist in the final few laps, sending him home in 3rd place. Jonathan is (at this writing) the current points leader on the Lucas Oil Late Model Dirt Series tour. He has won nine races in a row including, five in a row on the Lucas Oil Tour. The Longhorn Chassis Company might want to use an old beer slogan as their slogan, "Look Out For The Bull." After watching this young dirt warrior race, I see nothing but a bright future for Jonathan Davenport and the whole K&L race team.

BILLY OGLE JR.

Billy Ogle Jr. in his Calhoun Restaurants sponsored #201. (Photo provided by Nick Nicholson)

Knoxville Tennessee's Billy Ogle Jr. was born on August 17, 1964. Being born into a racing family sometimes has its advantages. Bill Sr. and his brothers Jim and Jack Ogles, at one time, owned both Atomic Speedway and the Smoky Mountain Speedway while young Billy Jr. was growing up. So it was only natural that

Billy Jr. would want to pursue a career in racing. However, it was not the type of racing career one would think. As a young boy, Billy wanted to race motorcycles for a living. Billy once told me, "Since my father owned dirt race car tracks at the time, it was easier for me to race cars, so I chose dirt cars over motorcycles in the end."

Over the years I have watched Billy race as a teenager in the street stocks, driving a '70 Plymouth Sebring and then a '55 Chevy, at Atomic Speedway. In 1980, he finished second in points and was named Street Stock Rookie of the Year in only his second year of racing. Billy ran limited late models for about a year then progressed to the late model ranks in 1982, winning Rookie of the Years honors in late models at Atomic. From a young teenager in street stocks to winning major racing events on the Lucas Oil and World of Outlaws national tours; I have watched Billy Ogle, Jr. develop into one of the best super late model drivers in the South.

Let's take a look at how he arrived at being the super late model driver he is today. In 1985 Billy joined forces with Harriman Tennessee's James Vanover, owner of Vanover Concrete Finishers. Ogle replaced Sherman Howell as the driver at Vanover Racing. This would develop into an almost 20 years Vanover-Ogle late model racing connection. The Calhouns Bar-B-Que Restaurants have been a major sponsor of Billy Ogle for a number of years. 1988 saw Billy win the first of what would be eight late model track championships at Atomic Speedway. The others being, '89, '90, '91, '93, '94, '95, '03. This is by far the most by a single driver in Atomic Speedway history, there are four drivers tied for second with three. In 1993 Ogles had one of his best years to date, winning track championships at both Atomic Speedway and the Crossville Raceway. He won a record 19 feature races at Atomic that year, including eight in a row.

Billy had a very successful season at the Tazewell (TN) Speedway in 1998. Ogle had a number of feature wins, including six in a row and was voted most popular driver at the track. However, this dwarfed in comparison to his Hav-A-Tampa Dirt Racing Series win in the 1998 Ray Neely Memorial 100. This was by far Ogle's biggest win to date. In 2002 Ogle teamed with Bill Reed on the UDTRA tour and won Rookie of the Year honors and finished 9th in points.

It was a race in 2005 that Billy said he had the best handling race car that he ever raced. The race was a 100 lap O'Reilly Auto Parts Southern All-Stars event at Atomic Speedway. Ogle started the race from 19th position and came through the field and into the lead very quickly. As the race was winding to the finish, Billy had lapped all but five of the cars in the field when he took the checkered flag in an easy win. After the race Ogle said, "This was a perfect race car tonight, I could put the car anywhere I wanted to, everyone that races should have a car like this just once."

In 2007 Ogle drove for up and coming late model driver, Petros Tennessee's Joe Armes. During his brief stint with Armes, Ogle won five events, including two Advance Auto Parts Thunder Series races and the Atomic Speedway Memorial race at Smoky Mountain Speedway.

Billy then began driving for Mike Kittrell Motorsports around 2008. In his three years with Mike he raced mostly regional races, including the Advance Auto Parts Thunder Series, finishing third in points. Ogle also won back to back (2009-10) Georgia Memorial races at Boyd's Speedway, along with several other feature wins. He also won the 2009 Tennessee Thunder Dirt Car Series championship.

After the three seasons driving for Kittrell Motorsports, Ogle teamed up with Maryville, Tennessee based Blount Motorsports, and its owner Larry Garner for the 2011 season. Billy won the 2011 Southern All-Stars Dirt Racing Series points championship the first season with his new team. The following year, Billy scored the biggest victory of his career when he won a Lucas Oil Late Model Dirt Series race at Volunteer Speedway, The Scorcher 50. Ogle not only won the race, he battled dirt racing king Scott Bloomquist almost the entire race, making a thrilling pass for the lead with only four laps to go to take the win. Billy would go on to win almost two dozen features and the 2014 Old Man's Garage Spring Nationals title in his almost four years of driving for the Garner team. However, the team experienced engine problems most of 2014. Ogle and Blount Motorsports parted ways after a disappointing showing at the World 100 that year at the Eldora Speedway.

Clinton Tennessee's Stacy Boles signed Billy to drive a second car for him in 2015. It appears Boles made the right decision. Billy appears to own the ultra fast Tazewell Speedway this year, scoring two major victories at the track. The first was a thrilling pass of Outlaw regular, Josh Richards coming out of turn four on the last lap to win the April 11th World of Outlaws Series race; taking Jimmy Owens with him, leaving Richards in their dust to finish third. Ogles pocketed a cool $10,000 payday for one of his biggest career wins. A little over two weeks later, on May 2nd Billy scored his second win in a row at the Taz, winning the $6,000 Old Man's Garage Spring Nationals race over Gray Court South Carolina's Chris Madden.

So as we have seen, if Billy Ogle, Jr. has the right racing equipment at his disposal, he can compete with the best super late model drivers in the country. So far in 2015, its appears he has found that equipment in Stacy Boles' Advanced Motorsports team.

RAY COOK

Ray Cook takes the #53 on a qualifying lap. (Photo provided bt Nick Nicholson)

I recently got a few minutes of Ray Cook's time to talk about his dirt racing career. This in itself was a major accomplishment. Cook is perhaps one of the busiest men in dirt racing today. Not only is this super late model driver, a threat to win anytime he shows up at a racing event; be it a $3,000 to win race at Boyds Speedway in Chattanooga, Tennessee, or the $41,000 Hillbilly 100 at Tyler County (WV) Speedway. In addition to racing, Cook also promotes three   super late model touring series during the racing season; the Schaeffer's Oil Southern Nationals, the Old Man's Garage Spring Nationals, and his newest series, the Southern Nationals Bonus Series. And if that were not enough, Ray is also the racing promoter at Tri-County Speedway in his hometown of Brasstown, North Carolina.

Ray Cook was born on September 29, 1971. He developed an interest in racing after watching his three cousins race in the street stock division at local tracks around his hometown. At the age of 15 his parents bought him a four-cylinder race car. Ray's racing career began in 1987, racing in the four cylinder division at Tri-County. His first of almost 200 career wins came in the four cylinders. In 1990 Cook purchased a used late model dirt car, and won the track championship at Blue Ridge Georgia's Sugar Creek Raceway. It took "the tarheel tiger" only a short time before he was racing super late models throughout the region. Cook also ran the Hav-A-Tampa (Xtreme) DirtCar Series from '96 until it ended in 2004 as the Stacker2 Xtreme DirtCar Series. Ray's best finish in the points standing was a fifth in his first year of '96.

The 2000 season started off with a bang for Cook. He was a winner at the STARS Winter Nationals at the East Bay (FLA) Raceway Park. However, the best was yet to come. Ray won the biggest race, at that time, of his career when he won the Show-Me 100 at West Plains (MO) Motor Speedway along with its $34,000 payday.

During the early 2000's Cook continued to race the Xtreme (HAT) Series and a number of regional races. In 2006, there was one Series that he was a regular driver in. That was the Southern Regional Racing Series, which ran from '06 until one race into '14. This was a very good regional series and I know Ray hated to see it end. Cook was the all time wins leader with 16 victories, winning at least one race in every year of the series. He also scored his first Lucas Oil Late Model Dirt Series win in '06 at Dixie Speedway in Woodstock, GA.

At one time in '05 Ray had a place next to my heart. I have always been a MOPAR fan from years past. In 2005 Cook piloted a Joe Gaerte Racing Engine Dodge on the super late model trail. I still remember the sound of that engine, it was just a different sound from a Ford or Chevy Engine. Just a "sweet" sound, thank you Ray Cook.

Cook continued to run in Southern All-Stars Racing events, winning at the old Toccoa (GA) Speedway in '08. He also continued racing in the SRRS. However, the year 2009 proved to be a good year for the "tarheel tiger." He won the biggest payday of his career; when he took the checkered flag in the famed Hillbilly 100 at the Tyler County (WV) Speedway, taking $41,000 back home to Brasstown, North Carolina with him.

Cook won his second Show-Me 100 in 2010. He also won two Lucas Oil Late model Dirt Series race in '10; winning at Bulls Gap Tennessee's Volunteer Speedway and at the Motorsports Park at Beckley, West Virginia. In 2011 Ray pick up two Carolina Clash Super Late Model wins, along with a $5,000 Southern All-Stars win at Cleveland (TN) Speedway. His biggest win of '11 was the UMP sanctioned Summer National victory at Paducah, KY. Cook scored another big money win in 2012 at the Swainsboro (GA) Raceway, taking the checkered flag and the $20,000 top prize in the Turkey 100.

During 2013 Ray had one of his best seasons, as far as wins go, winning 12 races. Those wins included, the NeSmith Chevrolet Dirt Late Model Series win at Bubba Raceway Park in Ocala, Florida. He continued to have success on the regional series trail, winning two Southern All-Stars and two Southern Regional Racing series races. He also won the annual "Boss" race at one of his favorite tracks, the Rome (GA) Speedway.

2014 saw Cook grab another NeSmith Chevrolet Dirt Late Model Series win, this time at Golden Isles (GA) Speedway. He also was a winner at the ultra fast Tazewell (TN) Speedway, in a

Southern National Bonus Series race, collecting a $5,000 check in victory lane.

In April of 2015, I saw Cook score an early win at Bull's Gap Tennessee's annual Spring Thaw. Ray lead all 50 laps in a win over Knoxville Tennessee's Billy Ogle Jr. In May of this year, at the Smoky Mountain Speedway, Ray started the $10,000 World of Outlaw event along side Scott Bloomquist on the outside of the front row. Scott took the lead and led all 50 laps for the win. However, Cook maintained his second place position for the entire 50 laps, beating Darrell Lanigan, Tim McCreadie, and a number of other World of Outlaw and Lucas Oil regulars.

Look for Ray Cook to become a dominant force in the super late racing. I feel Ray has a bright future ahead of him. Maybe winning one of Eldora's famed racing events, either the World 100 or The Dream. How about both?

DALE MCDOWELL

Dale McDowell piloting the #17M just after a race. (Photo provided by Nick Nicholson)

Rossville Georgia's Dale McDowell was born May 18, 1966. He started his racing career in 1980, competing in the hobby division at the Cleveland (TN) Speedway about 30 miles up the road from his hometown. After only a couple of years in the hobbies, McDowell decided to give late model racing a try in '83. Dale's first race in the late model division was a checkered flag at Cleveland. Since that first late model win, McDowell has gone on to make a name for himself in the world of super late model dirt racing.

For many years after his first late model win, McDowell was a frequent   winner throughout the region. However, Dale decided that in order to take his racing career to the next level, he must start traveling. One of the first touring series he was involved with was the Southern All-Stars Racing series in the late 80's. Dale finished second to Ronnie Johnson in the SAS points in 1988. The next year he won 2 of the 13 races on the SAS schedule. The next few years saw him in victory lane several times in the SAS, and he won the series points championship in '94.

In 1990, McDowell started competing on his first national dirt touring series, the (Xtreme) Hav-A-Tampa Dirt Racing Series. He was very successful on the tour, winning the Hav-A-Tampa Shootout at Dixie (GA) Speedway in 1999 and again in 2001. Dale had a nine win season in '02, and is second on the all-time wins list with 31 victories.

Dale said one of his all time memorable moments in racing was winning the Hav-A-Tampa Series Point Championship in '99. His primary sponsor, Bob Harris, left McDowell and his team in mid-season, citing the excessive amount of travel involved with the series as his reason for leaving. This left Dale and his crew chief/ brother Shane McDowell to put together their own program for the rest of the season; with some help from associate sponsor, O.J. Monday. They were right in the middle of a heated points battle with Batesville Arkansas' Wendell Wallace. The first of the season had gone really well for McDowell's team. Although they scored fewer wins in the second half, they were consistent enough to keep close in the points chase. As the races wound down, Wallace went into the season ending Shootout leading by 31 points. What made the title chase more interesting was the fact that both drivers were sponsored by O.J. Monday Trucking Company out of Hot Springs, Arkansas. However, an ill-handling race car would cost Wallace the points tile. McDowell would go on to win the Shootout and beat out, 12th place finisher, Wallace for the points title by 22 points. Because of the way the season had gone, Dale said from victory lane, "This is a dream come true."

McDowell had another memorable win in 2000. That year NASCAR's Bristol Speedway was turned into a dirt track for the inaugural UDTRA's "Battle of Bristol" super late model dirt race. Mike Balzano was leading the race when he broke a wheel. This gave the lead to McDowell, who went on to win the race over his old rival Wendell Wallace. He said this win ranked right up there with his Hav-A-Tampa Shootout win. Dale continued to compete on the UDTRA/Hav-A-Tampa series, finishing fourth in points in'01; second in points in '02; and sixth in points in '03.

Dale drove for Larry Shaw Race Cars out of Batesville, Arkansas, from 2001 until 2006. He had a number of big wins during his time with the Rocket racing chassis builder. Some of those victories were, the '01 Bama Bash at Green Valley (ALA) Speedway; the $12,000 James King Memorial in '04, at Columbus (MS) Speedway; Batesville Arkansas Speedway's "Topless 100" in '04; the '01 and '05 USA Nationals at Cedar Lake (WI) Speedway; and the '06 National 100 at the famed East Alabama Motor Speedway in Phenix City, Alabama. Also while driving for Shaw, he won the World 100 at the legendary Eldora Speedway in 2005. McDowell was awarded the win after Shannon Babb was found to be 10 pounds light at the scales. But hey, a win is a win.

In '08 Dale McDowell Racing won their second Bama Bash in the super late model division. Dale also won the crate late model division that year, driving for a fellow driver. During the '08 and '09 seasons the team raced a Goddard Warrior racing chassis. Later, McDowell was the driver for NASCAR's Clint Bowyer for the '10 thru the '12 seasons. Dale had three wins in 2010, including a $5,000 victory at Lakeside (KS) Speedway over teammate Jared Landers. In 2011 he had another $5,000 win at North Georgia Speedway in Chatsworth, Georgia.

Currently McDowell drives for Team Dillon Racing and had perhaps the best season of his racing career in 2014. He ran a limited racing schedule for the season. Dale competed in 36 races with, 8 Checkered flags, 18 top five finishes, and 25 top 10's. This included, winning the $10,000 Lucas Oil Late Model Dirt Series' "Scorcher 50" at the Volunteer Speedway at Bulls Gap, Tennessee. But his biggest career win came in the $100,000 "Dream" 100 at Eldora. Dale Said it was great to finally celebrate in Eldora's Victory Lane. He is only the sixth driver to win both the "World 100" and "The Dream."

Today, Dale is a major force in the dirt super late model ranks. He is also quite busy with other interests outside of driving his Team Dillon Racing #17M. McDowell is also part owner of Boyd's Speedway in Chattanooga, Tennessee, along with National Boiler Service owner David Duplissey. Even with those two commitments, Dale somehow still finds time to run a late model driving school at Boyds Speedway. I feel you are going to hear a lot more of Team Dillon and "McDaddy" in the coming years.

RONNIE JOHNSON

Ronnie Johnson at Boyd's Speedway in his familiar #5. (Photo provided by Nick Nicholson and Ronnie Johnson)

Ronnie Johnson was born on December 17, 1955 in Chattanooga, Tennessee into a racing family that included his father, the legendary NASCAR driver and former owner of the Cleveland (TN) Speedway, Joe Lee Johnson. His father was a strict parent, and Ronnie was not allowed to race until a week after graduating high school in June of 1973. After winning his first race, which was a heat race, at the Cleveland Speedway in 1974; Johnson quickly got the hang of winning, and continues to be one of the top dirt late model drivers in the country.

While growing up, Ronnie said there was never any doubt as to the career he would choose. Johnson told me, "Being around racing with my dad at the shop and in the pits, as a kid, I just naturally wanted to be like some of the great drivers I was watching, like Bud Lunsford, Snooks Defore, Leon Brindle, and Charles Hughes." He went on to say, "I especially looked up to Hughes and the incredible seasons he was having in '76 (winning the World 100) and '77."

During the 80's Johnson ran mostly in the East Tennessee area at tracks like, Kingsport, Atomic, Smoky Mountain, and Boyd's, with a lot of success. For example, he won a total of 38 Features in 1986 alone. Johnson said, "Atomic Speedway remains my favorite track because of all the great wins I had there over the years."

Throughout his long career, Johnson has run his share of dirt touring series races. However, the Southern All-Stars Dirt Series is perhaps the only one he has competed in for the points championship. Ronnie has won three titles in that series, 1985, '87, and '88. The 1990's saw Ronnie score two of his biggest wins, two Dirt Track World Championships at the Legendary Pennsboro Speedway in 1992 and again in '94. Otherwise, Johnson has ran pretty much an "outlaw" racing schedule. Ronnie said, "I've heard many times over the years, in racing it takes $125 to make a $100." He told me, "I race where its most beneficial to me, in terms of both, costs and the return." Ronnie continued, "If I can race closer to home for a few thousand dollars less, then I stand a chance of making just as much, if not more, than if I traveled long distances and had larger expenses, which would take away from my winnings."

Ronnie has driven for a number of good racing teams and sponsors over the years. Among them were, Bob Miller, and his

Miller Bros. Construction Co. and Hawkeye Trucking Co., from 1989 til 1995. In the early 80's he was teamed with Race Engine Design. Shadden Trucking Co., and West Alabama Paving were also major sponsors for Johnson in the 80's. It was in 1996, that Ronnie ran a second Bloomquist car for a year for dirt racing legend, Scott Bloomquist.

In the late 90's and into the 2000's, sponsorship money was not easily obtained. With the high costs of racing (especially engines) Johnson could no longer afford to stay on the road for weeks at the time. During this time, he was racing a number of local races and low profile special event races throughout the Georgia, Tennessee, and Alabama areas. Ronnie has raced for a number of car owners since the 2000's began, among them were, Scott Russell, Chuck Smith, and Rocket chassis' Sanford Goddard.

In 2005, as Johnson's search for sponsors and money to run his racing operation appeared to be drying up, along comes a career saving new series. Mike Vaughn of Cartersville, Georgia introduced the Crate Racin' USA Series. Vaughn came up with a traveling late model dirt series in which he would cut engine costs drastically. He proposed the use of a Cheverolet Performance 604 Circle Track engine. This engine would be factory sealed to prevent any expensive high dollar aftermarket modifications and would cost around $5,000. This is a very affordable late model race engine by today's standards. Most of today's super late model engines range from the $40,000 range of a Cornett all the way to around $62,000 for a Roush Yates (RY45). In spite of the hardships Johnson was facing, 2010 was one of the beat seasons of his forty plus years of racing. He won an amazing 28 races and had 54 top 5 finishes in his 68 starts that year.

Suddenly, Ronnie's racing career gained new life, Chevrolet signed him to a contract as their research and development driver. Now Johnson was not only winning races on the NeSmith Dirt Late Model Series (formerly the Crate Racin' USA Series); he was giving valuable feedback on the 604 engine, as well as the new CT 525 engine for super late models. The CT 525 race engine is an all-aluminum engine and was similar to the LS3 Chevy engine that was found in the Chevrolet Corvette. It too was factory sealed to cut down on racing costs, with a price tag of around $10,000.

Since joining the NeSmith series, Ronnie has won the 2013 and 2014 NeSmith Late model National Championship. In 2014, he also won the new Chevrolet Performance Super Late Model Series National Championship and the $10,000 that went along with that award. As of 2014 Johnson was the NeSmith Late Model career wins leader, with 25 victories.

Ronnie has won somewhere in the neighborhood 600 races during his long and successful career. Johnson was given the ultimate honor a driver can receive in dirt racing 2004, when he was inducted into the National Dirt Late Model Hall of Fame. In 2011, his late father and mother, Joe Lee and Jean Johnson were recognized by the Hall of Fame as contributors to the sport as promoters. Fittingly the whole family is now a part of the Hall.

One thing Ronnie's race fans and competitors have grown accustom to over the years is, never expect Ronnie Johnson to show up on time for a race. He has said, "I always work hard on my race car during the week, and its ready to race when I get to the track." So always look for his 30+ year old converted furniture trailer rig, with the famous Chevrolet bow tie on its side; to show up sometime before the race starts. But never count Ronnie out, even if he has to start in the rear of the field. He has won from there before.

STEVE "HOT ROD" LaMANCE

Steve "Hot Rod" LaMance in one of his Hot Rod #8 late models. (Photo provided by Nicholson)

Steve "Hot Rod" LaMance is another of those drivers, like Ronnie Johnson, who has enjoyed a very long and successful career in late model dirt racing. Another thing that makes these two veteran dirt warriors somewhat alike; is the fact that both their racing careers got a jump start by being introduced to a new late model touring series at just the right time. As both were thinking that their driving days were winding down. Along comes a new late model racing series to rekindle their desire to continue competitive dirt racing. In Ronnie Johnson's case, it was the NeSmith Dirt Late Model Series that gave his career new life. However, it was a series called the FASTRAK Pro Late Model Series that helped revive LaMance's desire to continue his dirt racing career.

Six Mile South Carolina's Steve "Hot Rod" LaMance was born on June 28, 1952. He has been racing the dirt tracks of Georgia, South Carolina, and North Carolina since 1976. Lamance began his career in the Rookie Class on the high banks of the Toccoa (GA) Speedway, and later on the red clay of Golden Strip Speedway in Fountain Inn, South Carolina. It took "Hot Rod" only a short time before he scored his first win that same year, driving his '68 Dodge Super Bee race car. Once LaMance started to win that year, he won races at tracks all over the region. In Addition to Toccoa and Golden Strip, Hot Rod scored wins at Anderson (SC) Motor Speedway, and the Riverside Speedway at Traveler's Rest, South Carolina. He has gone on to see several hundred checkered flags in his 40 year racing career as one of the South's best late model dirt warriors.

Hot Rod won the annual Shrine race at Toccoa Speedway in one of his last races in the Rookie class. Later, he raced for a short time in the Cadet class. In 1978, LaMance started driving for Ben Durham in the Limited Late Model Division at Gaffney South Carolina's Cherokee Speedway. LaMance won his first race for Durham at the historic track. They had several other feature wins that year at tracks throughout the region. In 1980 Durham built a Chevy Camaro and the team won seven out of eight races at Toccoa, causing the track to put a bounty on LaMance.

Carolina Tool Company came on board as the sponsor of the Ford Mustang for the Durham/LaMance race team in '81. This Mustang became a crowd favorite among Ford fans at Cherokee

Steve "Hot Rod" LaMance sitting in his #85 before a FASTRAK race at Toccoa Speedway. (Photo provided by the author)

Speedway where it was almost unbeatable. Hot Rod had several wins that year at Cherokee. This resulted in LaMance winning the first ever track championship for Ford. In '82 Hot Rod started driving for Jack Finley, with Carolina Tool remaining as the primary sponsor.

The first and only South Carolina Dirt Track Outlaw Championship was held in 1983. LaMance said this was one of his all-time favorite races. He said it was based on local track points, pitting Lower State drivers against the Upper State drivers. Hot Rod won the race with ease, beating some of the best late model drivers in South Carolina in the process. He told me the race was very popular among both the fans and drivers. LaMance said, "To this day I still wonder why the race ended after that one year." The next three years saw Hot Rod drive race cars mainly for himself. During the time, he had several wins at tracks that included, Laurens (SC) Speedway, Hartwell (GA) Speedway, and the Cherokee Speedway.

1986 saw Hot Rod again team up with car owner Ben Durham. The two picked up right where they had left off, winning five of seven races at the end of the '86 season. The rest of the 80's were very successful for LaMance and Durham. In '87, they had a number of wins at, I-85 Speedway, Riverside Speedway, and the

Cherokee Speedway. LaMance had 25 victory Lane appearances in 1988. He split his driving duties in 1989, scoring 14 wins in limited late models, and an amazing 27 wins in super late models.

LaMance teamed up with the Young brothers at the start of the 90's. He again became a crowd favorite when he started driving another Ford late model. Hot Rod had several victory lane appearances all over the region. Those included wins at, Sugar Creek Speedway in Union, South Carolina, Riverside Speedway, Laurens Speedway, and the Cherokee Speedway. During the early 90's, Cherokee Speedway started running two super late model races per night. They were known as the "Twin 25's." The first race was started straight up, the fastest on the pole. The second race was always inverted, the winner of the first race starting in the rear. This was very popular among the fans at Cherokee Speedway because it was hard to win both races. LaMance was very successful during this time at Cherokee. He usually won at least one of these races, sometimes he did win both. A bonus of $2,000 was paid if both races were won by the same driver. In 1991, Hot Rod won both races at the "Peach Festival Race" at Cherokee. This win, along with several other wins that year, helped LaMance win his second Cherokee Late Model Points Championship. Like his first track championship in 1981, Hot Rod won this one too in a Ford.

In addition to his two points championships at Cherokee, Hot Rod has also won four Track Championships at Riverside (SC) Speedway. Those were, '82, '91, '05, and '06. He also won the points title at the Lavonia (GA) Speedway in 2002. In the early 2000's, LaMance drove a GRT race car for Max Miller. Together they won several races throughout Georgia, South Carolina, and even into North Carolina. One winning streak included, 11 wins in 13 starts. He continued to win races over the next couple of years.

In the early 2000's, his team like so many others, were experiencing the dramatic increase in the costs of race engines. Hot Rod said, "It was taking the fun, along with a number of race teams, out of super late model racing." Around 2004, LaMance was introduced to the FASTRAK Racing Series, located in Carnesville, Georgia. This series was about to have a dramatic impact on the veteran dirt warriors future in late model dirt racing.

Hot Rod has scored over 30 FASTRAK Series wins and, in 2006, was the first $50,000 FASTRAK Grand National winner. He has scored a number of those wins at Lavonia (GA) Speedway. He wins so often there that he is sometimes called, "Lavonia LaMance." He continues to win FASTRAK races in the region at a steady clip. He won Lavonia Speedway's annual "Charlie Mize Memorial Race" in July of 2014, over a star studded field of FASTRAK drivers that included NASCAR's Kenny Wallace. He also won two Pro Late Model Championships at Westminister (SC) Speedway and Toccoa (GA) Speedway in 2012. In 2014, he was Lavonia's FASTRAK Points Champion.

LaMance said, "I just appreciate all FASTRAK has done, not just for me, but for racing in general." Hot Rod said, 'This crate engine series has allowed a lot of teams to continue to race and have fun at the same time. The series takes care of the drivers and gives the race fans a great show. I see it continuing to grow in the coming years."

I have known Hot Rod LaMance since the early 80's, watching him race in the FASTRAK series recently, I can tell you he is having one of the best times of his career. Don't expect this veteran late model driver to hang up the racing suit or put down the racing helmet any time soon. Why do that, when you are having so much fun doing what you love.

SKIP ARP

You would probably have to look a long time to find a more likable super late model dirt driver than Georgetown Tennessee's Skip Arp. He was born in the tiny Georgetown community on April 5, 1963. In 1978, his mother and father, Jeanette and Pete, were responsible for helping young Arp get his start in dirt racing. In the early years of his career, Skip's dad helped quite a bit on his early race cars. The first one being a Chevy Corvair, given to him by a friend. Arp scored his first late model victory at the Cleveland (TN) Speedway in 1981.

The first few years of Skip's late model career, saw him compete close to home at the Cleveland Speedway, and Boyd's

Skip Arp powers through a turn at Boyd's Speedway. (Photo provided by Skip Arp)

Speedway in Chattanooga, Tennessee. Later, White Oak Mountain Trucking's, Jackie and Linda Williams became one of Arp's first sponsors. With this new sponsorship he was able to start competing at other tracks in the region; like the Sugar Creek Raceway in Blue Ridge, Georgia; Atomic Speedway near Knoxville, Tennessee; and the Volunteer Speedway at Bull's Gap, Tennessee.

In 1988 Arp would land a sponsorship the would put him on the national stage in late model dirt racing. He would team with Ralph Curtis, owner of the Curtis Equipment Sales, out of Loudon, Tennessee. They would have a thirteen year racing relationship that would see them compete successfully in the Hav-A-Tampa Dirt Racing Series (Xtreme). Arp ran the series from 1991 until the series ended in 2004. His first series win was at Bulls Gap Tennessee's Volunteer Speedway on June 7, 1991; and his last series win was at Chatsworth Georgia's North Georgia Speedway on April 26, 2003. Skip's best year in the series was '98, when he had 5 wins and finished second in the points to Scott Bloomquist. He is 9th on the Hav-A-Tampa's all time wins list with 14 wins. However, his biggest career win came in the UDTRA (Hav-A-Tampa) race at Atomic (TN) Speedway on September 1, 2002, when he took home the $20,000 payday.

Curtis and Arp decided to end their relationship at the start of the '02 season.

It was during this time that two important events occurred in Skip's racing career. First, Greenbrier Arkansas' Joe Garrison hired Arp as a technical consultant for his GRT racing chassis company. Then he joined Donnie Crowder and "Buck Shot" McCall's Cromac racing team out of Lauren, SC. He raced with Cromac Racing for a few years and parted ways at the end of the '05 Season.

Stanley Best Heating and Air out of Maryville, Tennessee came on board as Arp's major sponsor in 2005. A short time later, Ralph Curtis also came back as a sponsor in '06. Stanley Best is still Skip's major sponsor today. They have a very close racing relationship and are planning to finish out Arp's career together.

During the last ten years, Skip has scored a number of wins in the Southern All-Stars Dirt Racing Series. His first checkered flag was at the Volunteer Speedway on April 22, 2000; and his last SAS victory was at the Cleveland (TN) Speedway on May 12, 2012. Skip Has scored other SAS wins at North Georgia Speedway, Atomic Speedway, and Dixie (GA) Speedway. He is Currently 18th on the SAS all time wins list with 9 victories. Another series Arp competed in was the old Southern Regional Racing Series. Skip had three wins in that series, all at Boyd's Speedway. Also, beginning with the 2000 season, Arp and fellow late model driver Freddy Smith operated a late model driving school at the Atomic Speedway for a few years.

Throughout his racing career, Skip has competed in several of Eldora's famed races, the World 100 and The Dream. He told me his best Eldora finish was a third in one of the World 100's. He has also won major races in a number of states including, Florida, Georgia, Tennessee, Pennsylvania, Kentucky, South Carolina, and Wisconsin. Today, Skip is closing in on 300 wins for his career.

In recent years, Arp has cut back on his racing schedule. However, he is still very competitive and a threat to win any race he enters. This was seen in a recent heat race win at Smoky Mountain Speedway's Lucas Oil Late Model Dirt Series race on June 20, 2015. I don't see him hanging up the racing uniform anytime soon. In 2008, The National Dirt Late Model Hall of Fame awarded the Sportsman Award to Georgetown Tennessee's Skip Arp. Like I said, "The Skipper" is one of the nicest super late model drivers you will ever meet in the world of dirt racing.

GARY MCPHERSON

Gary McPherson waits for the start of a race. (Photo provided by Gary McPherson)

I have known Gary for about 25 years and one thing can be said about this super late model driver from North Georgia; give him the right racing equipment he can run with the top drivers of the sport on any given night. Gary McPherson was born in Detroit, Michigan on October 30, 1956. Gary moved South to Dalton, Georgia when he was nine years old. Even from an early age he was fascinated with cars, helping his uncles in their auto shops.

Gary started his racing career by racing go-karts at an early age. Around the age of 16, he decided to give stock car racing a try. Gary started racing a 1965 Ford in the hobby divisions at the local tracks around his home town of Dalton. McPherson has moved on to race late models and then super late models for over forty years. He works on and maintains his race cars at his automotive shop, located on Downing Street in Dalton. Since he has no major sponsors like most of the touring drivers in the sport. Gary looks to a number of local sponsors to help fund his racing program, like longtime sponsor Carpet Discount Center. Others sponsors over the years have included, Apex Samples, Dale Yarn Sales, and Lofty's Textile Waste. McPherson relies on his long time crew chief, Danny Hedrick, who handles most of the work involving the cars cosmetic work and race setups. Others who lend a hand in the pits are, Lisa and Robby Hedrick, Jerry Bradley, Kelly Cantrell, Donny Hedrick; and Gary's wife, Dorothy who keeps the records for the team. McPherson is the person in the operation who keeps on top of the engine program. Also, he has raced several racing chassis over the years, such as C. J. Rayburn, and Mastersbuilt. However, one of the racing chassis he is currently running is a Scott Bloomquist Racing Chassis. Over the years, Gary has always been a master at choosing the right tires for a race. He told me, "I prefer the no tire rule at a race track. I always seem to do better at those tracks."

Some of McPherson's racing accomplishments include; a number of major event wins at the Cleveland (TN) Speedway like; the Miller 50 in '87; the Jean Johnson Memorial in '88; and the Independence holiday race known as, Stars and Stripes 50 in '93. Gary also won the $3,000 to win Boss 100 at the big half-mile, Rome (GA) Speedway in 2007. However, his two biggest accomplishments occurred at his home track, North Georgia Speedway, located in Chatsworth, Georgia. The first was his big 1993 Hav-A-Tampa Series win over, Skip Arp, Dale McDowell, and a top field of late model drivers. Finally, McPherson has one record that he is very proud of; the sixteen track Championships he earned at North Georgia, including winning seven in a row from '90 to '96. Some of Gary's best years were the '93 and '98 seasons. McPherson has claimed around 300 checkered flags during his four decades long racing career. This includes; wins at Atomic (TN) Speedway; Dixie Speedway in Woodstock, GA; the Rome (GA) Speedway; and several wins over the years at the North Georgia Speedway.

As long as he still enjoys racing, I don't see him putting down the racing helmet anytime soon. Gary McPherson is a very good super late model driver, a good person, and a friend.

AARON RIDLEY

Aaron Ridley coming out of a turn during qualifying. (Photo provided by Nick Nicholson)

Aaron Ridley was born in Chatsworth, Georgia on June 22, 1985. Aaron is a member of the famous Ridley racing family. His cousin being the legendary Jody Ridley, who for years dominated both the asphalt and dirt short tracks of the South.

I have known young Ridley since he was a teenager racing go-karts with his dad, Doug Ridley. My son, Gary Jr., was also racing go-karts at the same time. He only raced Aaron once at North Georgia Mini Speedway's first ever race in the mid-'90's. Aaron was a tough competitor. However, my son had the good fortune of winning that day. After my son left kart racing, I watched Ridley during his later karting days. Seeing him score a number of wins, I knew he had the talent necessary to enter the very competitive world of late model dirt racing.

By 2002 Aaron had indeed started a dirt racing career, driving the #8 dirt sportsman race car for Jody Ridley Motorsports, out of his hometown of Chatsworth, GA. In '03 Ridley moved to the dirt late models, still racing with Jody's motorsports team. It was at this time that Aaron changed his racing number to his familiar #81. During the '03 season Aaron continued to gain valuable experience in late model dirt racing. It was in the Fall of that year that he scored what was perhaps the biggest win of his young career. On September 7, 2003, he won the Hicks Specialty Welding 50 at his home track at North Georgia Speedway. He took the checkered flag with its $5,000 top prize over a star studded field that included, Ray Cook, Ronnie Johnson, and David Payne.

In '05 Ridley decided to try running in a new series called, the Tennessee Thunder DirtCar Series. His consistent finishes earned him Rookie of the Year honors, and a 2nd place finish in the series points that year.

Another series came onto the dirt racing scene in 2009 called, the National All Star Racing Association. Aaron decided to compete in the series' inaugural season. It proved to be a good decision, Ridley won the series' first Point Championship that year; edging out Campbellsville, Kentucky's Justin Radcliff. In 2010 Aaron won his 2nd Points Championship. He also scored a big series win at Richmond (KY) Raceway on September 4, 2010. He won two of the series' three championships before the series ended in 2011.

Aaron ran a select racing schedule in 2011, earning a win in the in the Pro Dirt Car Series at Talladega (ALA) Short Track. Ridley also raced in the 2011 Lucas Oil Dixie Shootout, at the famed

Dixie Speedway in Woodstock, GA. Aaron had a productive weekend, winning his heat race. He would then go on to finish a very respectable 6th in a race that late model superstar, Scott Bloomquist would win.

2012 proved to be one of the best seasons of Ridley's young career. Aaron raced quite a bit on Southern Regional Racing Series schedule, finishing 5th in the series points battle. He also scored three series wins. Those victories were at North Georgia Speedway, Sugar Creek Raceway, and Boyd's Speedway. Aaron said, "The win at North Georgia was one of the best races at the speedway in quite some time." He said, "The last 20 laps were some side by side racing with Riley Hickman for the lead." This was a big win for Aaron since he started his racing schedule later than usual in 2012. Maybe he should start his schedule late every year. During the 2012 season, Ridley ran a total of 35 races and never finished out of the top 10 in any of them.

Aaron started 2013 off with a bang, winning the Ice Bowl Championship at Talladega (ALA) Short Track in the limited late model division. He also won two steel-head late model races at North Georgia Speedway. However, his biggest win of the '13 season was his Ray Cook's Shaeffer Oil Southern Nationals victory. Aaron defended his North Georgia Speedway home turf. Ridley started from the inside pole and lead all 35 laps of the race. He took the Checkered flag and the $3,500 win over Knoxville Tennessee's Billy Ogle Jr.

The 2014 Season saw Ridley run a number of races in both, the super late model and limited late model divisions. Aaron raced several Southern All-Stars Racing Series events in '14. In the 3rd annual SAS B.J. Parker Memorial, he came from his 10th starting spot to finish 7th in a super late model field loaded with stars. The late Fall saw Aaron again have a good SAS finish in the annual Gobbler Race at Cleveland (TN) Speedway. He finished 5th in the race that was won by the newly crowned 2014 Southern All-Stars Point Champion, Riley Hickman.

The 2015 Sweetheart Race, at Seymour Tennessee's 411 Motor Speedway, started Ridley's current season off with a bang. Aaron started on the pole and won the late model event over Pierce Mc-Carter; who charged from mid-pack to finish second in the event.

Aaron is one of the up and coming young stars of super late model dirt racing. Look for him to have a successful racing career on many of the South's clay ovals.

RILEY HICKMAN

Riley Hickman's Super late model at Boyd's Speedway. (Photo provided by the author)

Riley Hickman was born on September 16, 1978 in his home-town of Cleveland, Tennessee. Hickman is another of those young super late model drivers that I've had the privilege of meeting during his go-kart racing days in the 90's. Hickman competes in steel head late model, and the crate late model divisions quite often. However, his main focus appears to be with the super late models.

The first few years of Hickman's late model career were spent racing locally, at the Cleveland (TN) Speedway and Boyd's Speedway in Chattanooga, TN. It was at Boyd's where he scored his first career win. I first saw Riley in a super late model in October of 2010. He was competing in the "Grant Adcox Memorial" Southern Regional Racing Series event at the Cleveland Speedway. Riley would take the victory over a very good field of super late models. Local racer Skip Arp finished second; followed by the "Tarheel Tiger" Ray Cook; Oak Creek Wisconsin's Dan Schleiper, and North Carolina's David Payne. It was that race that convinced me, Hickman had the ability to become the super late model driver he has today.

As mentioned, Riley has taken several checkered flags over the years in steel head and crate late models. Those wins include, 2014's the "King of the Gap" win at Volunteer Speedway and its $4,000 payday. He also had another big steel head win in '14 at North Georgia Speedway. The early part of 2015 has seen him add, two steel head and two crate late model wins to his total. The two crate wins this year were United Crate Racing Alliance sanctioned events.

Hickman has started to make a name for himself in super late model racing in the region. He has become one of the drivers to beat on the Southern All-Stars Dirt Racing Series. Riley has won the series points championship in 2013, and again in 2014. Being consistent was the key to winning his '13 title; while his first three series wins in'14, helped him win last years title. Hickman was in victory lane in 2014 at Boyd's Speedway's SAS $5,000 to win "Shamrock 50" on March 22. He won the last two series races of the year at, the Talladega Short Track on October 18; and at his home track at the Cleveland Speedway on November 21. Riley is currently (as of June 20th) leading the series points for 2015.

Another regional series he won the points title in was the Southern Regional Racing Series, which ran from 2006, until it ended after one race in 2014. Riley won the SRRS points Championship in 2012. During the series he had four wins; including a win in the series' last race on February 8, 2014, at Boyd's Speedway. Finally, Hickman has competed in Carnesville Georgia's Ultimate Super Late Model Series, winning a series race at Lavonia (GA) Speedway in 2013.

His biggest career win came in October of 2014 in a Southern Nationals Bonus Series race. The race was at Duck River Raceway Park at Wheel, Tennessee. Riley won the "Deep Fried 75," leading the entire 75 laps in winning the $11,000 payday over Dale Mc-Dowell and Steve Casebolt.

Since teaming with "Urkel," (Brad Carvin-crew chief) Hickman has gained the confidence and consistency necessary to become a threat to win at any race he enters. I see Hickman becoming a force in the region in super late model dirt racing for years to come. Over the years, my son, Gary, and I bought a lot of go-kart parts from Riley and his late father. Riley has since gone on to become one of the best young men I know in dirt racing.

RANDY WEAVER

The red, white, and gold #116 of Randy "Dream" Weaver. (Photo provided by the author)

Another driver we need to mention, because of the "dream" season he is having in 2015, is Crossville Tennessee's Randy "Dream" Weaver. He along with K&L Racing's Jonathan "Superman" Davenport are two of the hottest super late model drivers in the country.

Randy has seen over 350 checkered flags during his career, which started in 1990. He is one of those super late model drivers who is currently running an "outlaw" racing schedule for the 2015 season. He has won races in a number of racing series in '15. Weaver is a frequent competitor on the Southern All Stars Dirt Racing Series. He has three SAS Points Championships to his credit and is approaching 30 wins on the tour. Other touring series where he has scored victories include, the Southern Regional Racing Series, Ultimate Super Late Model Series, Southern Nationals Series, Tennessee Thunder DirtCar Series, and the Spring Nationals Series.

Weaver has scored a number of big money, high profile wins. Some of those victories were, the 2005 Blue/Gray 100 at Gaffney South Carolina's legendary Cherokee Speedway, and the $15,000 Coor's Light Fall Classic at the Whynot (MS) Motorsports Park in 2014.

However, it is 2015 season that we want to mention here. Randy started the season off with eight straight feature wins. Those early wins include, a SAS $8,500 win at East Alabama Motor Speedway at Phenix City, Alabama; two Ultimate Super Late model Series wins, one of those a $20,000 win at Virginia Motor Speedway in Jamaica, Virginia. Others were, three more SAS wins, along with a Spring Nationals and Southern Nationals Bonus Series wins.

Randy has Started 15 races in 2015 (including June 20th). He now has nine wins, including his June 20th victory lane appearance at the Smokey Mountain Speedway in the Lucas Oil Late Model Dirt Series race. Weaver was on point for the Ole Smoky Moonshine Classic. Randy steadily worked his way to the front, taking the lead from pole sitter Chris Ferguson on lap 17 and was never really challenged after that. He won his first ever $10,000 Lucas Oil race over, Scott Bloomquist, and a hard charging Jonathan Davenport, who came from 10th starting position to finish a close third. This ended Davenport's nine race winning streak, five in a row on the Lucas Oil tour.

This was one hot 2015 driver cooling off another of the year's hottest super late model drivers. I have watched Randy's racing career progress through the years; from being a regular late model competitor and winning point championships at the high banked Crossville Raceway in the early 90's; to recently standing in the winner's circle at a national touring series event at Smoky Mountain Speedway. Look for the Randy Weaver to have a lot more big wins in the future in his familiar red, white and gold #116 super late model. Who knows, he may even decide to give the Lucas Oil regulars a "run for their money" in the series points championship soon.

This gives us an even "baker's dozen" for our look at some of today's late model dirt warriors. These drivers and many more are racing the dirt tracks of the South. They will continue to write their chapter in super late model dirt racing history in the years to come.

BACK OF THE BOOK PHOTOS

#1- Smoky Mountain Speedway a recent photo looking toward the first turn. Note how far down the straight-away the flag stand is. Track was shortened on the turns one and two side from its original half mile to its present 4/10 mile. (Photo provided by the author)

#2- Looking toward turn two at the Tazewell (TN) Speedway. You get an idea of the high banking of the track. (Photo provided by the author)

#3- Looking from the bottom of the grandstands toward the scoring tower at Rome (GA) Speedway. (Photo provided by the author)

#4- The new entrance to Boyd's Speedway in Chattanooga,TN. (Photo provided by the author)

#5- A view of the large grandstand area at the old Lakewood Speedway in Atlanta, GA during a Sunday afternoon race in the late 70's. That is Leon Sells #77 in the lead. (Photo provided by Leon Sells)

#6- An early 57 Chevy late model racing at Smoky Mountain Speedway in the 60's. (Photo provided by Robbie Henry)

#7- This is an early Pontiac late model during a race at Smoky Mountain Speedway in the 60's. (Photo provided by Robbie Henry)

#8- *An early modified race car of H.E. Vineyard's. (Photo provided by H.E. Vineyard)*

#9- *This is a young H.E. Vineyard with an early #24 Jalopy race car. (Photo provided by H.E. Vineyard)*

#10- A look at a classic skeeter race car being driven by Leon Sells. (Photo provided by Leon Sells)

#11- Jody Ridley in the Kozy Korner Cafe Special after just setting a new track record at Rome (GA) Speedway in the late 70's. (Photo provided by Jody Ridley)

#12- A photo taken in the late 70's at Rome (GA) Speedway. The cars are going into turn three for the start of a feature race. The first five race cars are, Charlie Mincy, Buck Simmons, Charles Hughes, Bud Lunsford, and Jody Ridley. Drivers ran without the hoods because the cars ran 10 to 20 degrees cooler without them. (Photo provided by Charlie Mincey)

#13- H.E. Vineyard sets a new world record at Atomic Speedway in Knoxville, TN. on August 4, 1979. Copy of an article in a newspaper. (Photo provided by David "Peanut" Jenkins)

#14- The Legendary Jeff Purvis #15, racing with H.E. Vineyard in the #24 at Atomic Speedway. (Photo provided by David "Peanut" Jenkins)

#15- H.E. Vineyard takes another checkered flag at Atomic Speedway in the Hawkeye Trucking Company #3 in the mid-80's. (Photo provided by H.E. Vineyard)

#16- "Little" Bill Corum takes a win at Atomic Speedway. (Photo provided by "Little" Bill Corum)

H.E. Vineyard Nips Buck Simmons
To Win NDRA Race At Volunteer

By WAYNE PHILLIPS
Assistant Sports Editor

Knoxville's H.E. Vineyard proved to local racing fans that he knows Volunteer Speedway's dirt oval about as well as he knows the steering wheel on his No. 24 Camaro after coming from behind to edge Buck Simmons by one-half car lengths and capture the $30,000 Looney Chevrolet 100 at Bulls Gap Saturday night.

Vineyard, a regular winner at Bulls Gap as well as other local dirt tracks, beat out the best names in the dirt racing business by coming from his ninth starting position to take the lead away from Simmons on the 86th lap and eke out the exciting win.

Simmons, the Baldwin, Ga., veteran, started the 100-lap event on the pole after setting a blistering qualifying speed of 15.57 on Friday night.

The National Dirt Racing Association (NDRA), sponsors of the event, altered their format somewhat by allowing the top seven qualifiers on Friday night to automatically make the starting field on Saturday. Normally only the top three qualifiers make the field without having to compete in a heat race.

But Vineyard, who qualified at 15.97, was not in that elite group of seven. He had to make the starting field by running in a heat race, which he easily won. When the main event started Saturday, Vineyard was sitting in the fifth row.

Freddie Smith of Kings Mountain, N. C., started alongside Simmons on the front row. Smith, driving a Camaro built by some Richard Petty "kinfolk," in Carolina, posted a qualifying speed of 15.58.

Smith jumped into the lead when the green flag fell on Saturday and kept it there until the 21st lap, when Simmons slipped underneath him in heavy traffic to take the lead. Smith later retired

drivers staged a terrific struggle the rest of the way, as most of the fans in the packed bleachers were on their feet to see the finish.

As the white flag came out to signify one lap remaining, Simmons moved alongside Vineyard in the first and second turns, but Vineyard pulled back ahead down the back straight. Coming off the fourth turn, Simmons made one final desperate lunge, roaring his machine within one-half car length of Vineyard as they bolted under the checkered flag.

Steve Smith wound up passing Helfrich and Bud Lunsford late in the race to take the third spot.

Drivers from throughout the south and north were on hand for the event. The top six qualifiers represented six different states: Simmons from Georgia, Freddie Smith from North Carolina, Larry Moore from Ohio, Helfrich from Indiana, Bobby Thomas from Alabama, and Jerry Inman from Mississippi.

A total of 28 cars started the race. The seven top qualifiers made it, then the top three cars out of six separate heat races which were staged Friday night advanced to the feature.

The final three spots in the starting field were earned by the top three finishers in a 50-lap consolation race which preceded Saturday's main event. Bill Morton of Church Hill won that consolation.

A 25-lap 6-cylinder race was also staged Saturday night, with Jonesboro's Bob Street coming out on top. Johnny Carr of Rogersville placed second, followed by Charles Byrd of Johnson City, Dave Bundren of Rogersville and John Doty of Greeneville.

OFFICIAL ORDER OF FINISH
NDRA Looney Chevrolet 100
1. H. E. Vineyard Knoxville No. 24

Roses To The Victor

H. E. Vineyard, left, of Knoxville wears the wreath of roses he received aft capturing the Looney Chevrolet 100 National Dirt Racing Association class Saturday night at Volunteer Speedway. Ralph Moore, Volunteer Speedw owner, offers his congratulations to the champ. Vineyard edged out Buck Si mons by a half-car-length in an exciting finish to the 100-lap race. (Sun photo Wayne Phillips)

#17- H.E. Vineyard scores an NDRA win at Volunteer Speedway in a close win over Buck Simmons in 1979. This is a copy of a newspaper article. (Photo provided by David "Peanut" Jenkins)

#18- Jack Boggs and Freddy Smith doing battle. (Photo provided by Nick Nicholson)

#19- Freddy Smith's crew getting his 00 ready for a race. (Photo provided by Nick Nicholson)

#20 Dewayne Hommel sliding through a turn. (Photo provided by Nick Nicholson)

#21- Leon Brindle in his Brindle Bros #38 Camaro at Cleveland (TN) Speedway. (Photo provided by Bobbi Dixon)

#22- Doug Kenimer getting straped in just before a race. Doug was a winner of the World 100 in 1977. (Photo provided by Paul's Auto Parts)

#23- Ronnie Johnson after winning the Michael Head Jr. Memorial in 2006. That is Mike Head with Ronnie. (Photo provided by Ronnie Johnson)

#24- Late model driver David Perry scores another win at Cherokee Speed-way in Gaffney, SC. David and his wife, Deborah, were promoters at the speedway in the mid-80's. (Photo provided by Deborah Perry)

#25- Clint Smith getting set to race in a O'Reilly's Southern All Star Race. (Photo provided by Nick Nicholson).

#26- The Flintstone Flyer powering through a turn during a race. (Photo provided by Nicholson)

#27- Mike Duvall (the Flintstone Flyer) ponders his next move during a pause in a race. (Photo provided by Nick Nicholson)

#28- Gary McPherson powers down the straight-away at North Georgia Speedway. (Photo provided by Nick Nicholson)

#29- Ray Cook getting in the #53. (Photo provided by Nick Nicholson)

#30- Ray Cook going on the track at Smoky Mountain Speedway for hot laps during a Lucas Oil race. (Photo provided by the author)

#31- Skip Arp at Smoky Mountain Speedway. (Photo provided by author)

#32- Jimmy Owens (In blue shirt) ponders his next set-up move on the #20. (Photo provided by the author)

#33- Billy Ogle is set to Qualify his #201 at Tazewell Speedway. (Photo provided by the author)

#34- Steve Francis preparing to Qualify at Smokey Mountain Speedway in June of 2015. (Photo provided by the author)

#35- Scott Bloomquist's crew getting his car ready at Smoky Mountain Speedway in June 2015. (Photo provided by the author)

#36- Scott Bloomquist waiting to hot lap at Smoky Mountain Speedway. (Photo provided by the author)

#37- Jonathan Davenport's car after his win at Cherokee Speedway in Gaffney SC, as it looked after just being unloaded at Smoky Mountain Speedway the next day. (Photo provided by the author)

#38- Jonathan Davenport after hot laps at Smoky Mountain Speedway in June 2015. (Photo provided by the author)

#39- Davenport's crew getting his #6 ready for a Lucas Oil Race. (Photo provided by the author)

#40- Buck Simmons and Doug Kenimer on the pole for the start of a race. Both are driving Camaros, the most popular race car during the time. Note this was before the snub nose cars that came later. (Photo provided by Paul's Auto Parts)

To order more copies of

Red Clay and Dust:

Copy this page, complete information, and mail with check or money order
to

Gary Parker, 1517 Maxwell Road, Chattanooga, TN 37412
423-580-2690 • eparker0923@gmail.com

Name _____

Shipping address _____

City_____State_____ Zip_____

Phone_____E-mail(optional for shipping confirmation)_____

Quantity _____ book(s) @ $24.95   = $ _____
Shipping first book   = $ ___5.00___
Shipping quantity _____ additional books @ $3.00   = $ _____
TN residents add sales tax @ .0925   = $ _____
                            TOTAL   = $ _____

- -

Name _____

Shipping address _____

City_____State_____ Zip_____

Phone_____E-mail(optional for shipping confirmation)_____

Quantity _____ book(s) @ $24.95   = $ _____
Shipping first book   = $ ___5.00___
Shipping quantity _____ additional books @ $3.00   = $ _____
TN residents add sales tax @ .0925   = $ _____
                            TOTAL   = $ _____

Mail completed form with check or money order to:
Gary Parker, 1517 Maxwell Road, Chattanooga, TN 37412
423-580-2690 • eparker0923@gmail.com

Hypatia Sans Pro and Georgia in SC on LSI 70# white
Type and design by Karen Paul Stone